AF712410

Changing TECHNOLOGY

OPPORTUNITY AND CHALLENGE

Changing TECHNOLOGY

OPPORTUNITY AND CHALLENGE

ALPHONSE F. TREZZA, Editor

A CONFERENCE SPONSORED BY THE FLORIDA STATE UNIVERSITY SCHOOL OF LIBRARY AND INFORMATION STUDIES AND THE CENTER FOR PROFESSIONAL DEVELOPMENT AND PUBLIC SERVICE

G. K. Hall & Co.
Boston

Changing Technology: Opportunity and Challenge

Alphonse F. Trezza

Copyright 1989
by G.K. Hall & Co.
70 Lincoln Street
Boston, Massachusetts 02111

All rights reserved.

No part of this book may be reproduced
without the written permission of the publisher.

Printed on acid-free paper and
bound in The United States of America.

Library of Congress Cataloging-in-Publication Data

Changing Technology: opportunity and challenge: proceedings of the fifth annual library conference, held March 8-11, 1987 / sponsored by Florida State University School of Library and Information Studies and the Center for Professional Development and Public Service; Alphonse F. Trezza, editor.

p. cm. -- (Professional librarian series)
ISBN 0-8161-1900-7 (pbk.)
ISSN 10406158
1. Library science--Technical innovations--Congresses.
2. Information technology--Congresses. 3. Libraries--Automation--Congresses. I. Trezza, Alphonse F. II. Florida State University. School of Library and Information Studies. III. Florida State University. Center for Professional Development and Public Service. IV. Series.
Z678.9.A1C46 1988 88-24491
025'.02'0285--dc19 CIP

Contents

Preface

The Fifth Annual Library Conference, sponsored by the Florida State University School of Library and Information Studies, and the Center for Professional Development and Public Service, convened 8 March 1987 on the campus of Florida State University in Tallahassee. The conference was planned and coordinated by Alphonse F. Trezza, professor, with the assistance and participation of the SLIS faculty and Dean F. William Summers. The theme of the Conference was "Changing Technology: Opportunity and Challenge."

Dean Summers opened the proceedings by introducing Bernard F. Sliger, president, Florida State University. President Sliger welcomed the conference attendees with brief remarks about the importance of librarians and information resources.

William J. Welsh, deputy librarian, Library of Congress, delivered the keynote address on "Libraries and Changing Technology." As the volume of printed material increases, the demands for storage space and the problems of preservation are continuing concerns for librarians. Welsh discussed the application of compact disc technology in the Library of Congress, including standards, selection, fee versus free access, and copyright. He also described the history and present status of deacidification and conservation/preservation of library collections. In his concluding remarks Welsh encouraged the participants to become aware of the implementation of modern technology in the world of information.

CHANGING TECHNOLOGY

Centralized and Distributed Databases: Is the Balance Tilting?

The Second General Session opened on Monday, 9 March, with Elisabeth Logan, assistant professor, FSU School of Library and Information Studies, presiding. M. E. L. Jacob, vice president, library planning, OCLC, addressed the topic "National Databases and Linkages." Jacob described three types of network linkages--VAN (Value Added Network), Gateways, and LSP (Linked Systems Project)--and the capabilities of each. Being the most recent development, LSP was discussed in more detail. This included the six issues of content and format, telecommunications, quality of service, system enhancement, staff skills, and economics. Jacob challenged the attendees to make systems work together for all libraries and to make them cost-effective for their clients.

Emily Gallup Fayen, assistant director for library systems, University of Pennsylvania, spoke on "Local Systems and Distributed Processing." Her presentation began with definitions of distributed processing. Fayen suggested that libraries are moving from a bibliographic utility model to a local systems model which would be more cost-effective and timely; however, it would have the drawback of having no union database. The needs for this conversion would be the bi-directional online transfer of records, the preservation of a central database for all to access the information, and the development of a common command language. Fayen suggested that libraries develop local systems, while maintaining unified national databases.

JoAn S. Segal, then executive director, Association of College and Research Libraries, ALA, provided a well-balanced view of "Peaceful Coexistence." Segal offered descriptions of three network configurations: the ring, the star, and the tree. Her analysis showed that the star is the most accurate and expedient. The ring, however, is the configuration preferred by most network users. In reality, there are no decentralized networks, because most are actually a mixture of the configurations. She also identified six levels of networking, from local to national, with examples and characteristics of each.

Proposed Information Age Commission, Technology and NCLIS

Alphonse F. Trezza, professor, FSU School of Library and Information Studies, presided over the Third General Session. He introduced Vivian Arterbery, Executive Director, National Commission on Libraries and Information Science. She spoke informally about the fifteen year history of NCLIS, and described its function as a catalyst for library concerns. NCLIS is sponsoring several programs that focus on literacy this year, including library services to children and to the elderly and cooperative programs with VISTA. Arterbery also elaborated on proposed legislation to establish an Information Age Commission and the stance which NCLIS has taken on this issue. In the final portion of this session, Arterbery and Trezza spoke on the prospect of a 1989 White House Conference and the need for legislative support in appropriating the necessary funds. (This presentation is not included in the proceedings as no prepared text was available.)

Tradition, Technology, and the Reference Function

Ida G. Adams, assistant director, Coleman Library, Florida Agricultural and Mechanical University, introduced the speaker for the Fourth General Session. Tina Roose, director, Reference Service, North Suburban Library System, Illinois, addressed the question, "How Can Online Database Searching Be Integrated into Traditional Reference Services?" She focused on how to create an environment for making online resources as readily available and easy to use as print materials. There are human, monetary, and physical barriers preventing the attainment of this goal. Finally, Roose discussed possible means for overcoming these barriers. In this day, our own philosophy is the only obstacle preventing librarians from successfully integrating online with traditional reference services.

The Fifth General Session, with Doris Clack, professor, FSU School of Library and Information Studies, presiding, continued the theme of "Tradition, Technology and the Reference Function." Karen Markey, assistant professor, School of Library Science, University of Michigan, explored "Improving the Accessibility of

Library Resources." After listing current developments and their impact on libraries, Markey elaborated on present and future applications of machine readable Library of Congress Subject Headings to improve the quality, consistency, and accuracy of subject cataloging and classification. Her final remarks touched on the negative and positive considerations which must be dealt with in order to augment reference services with new technology systems.

Dale Carrison, director, Minnesota State University System/Program for Automated Library Systems, talked about "The Online Catalog: Reference/User Friend or Foe." Carrison surmised that library automation is a necessity for all libraries and that access by users should not depend on their knowledge of cataloging rules. In the past, libraries have forced users to follow their analytical methods for locating information, even though user terms did not always match the library's controlled vocabulary. Today's online catalogs should have access and retrieval capabilities beyond those of the traditional card catalog.

The stimulating topic "Staffing the New Technology Reference Desk," was addressed by Kathleen Prendergast, manager, information services, Northwestern University. She focused on the role of the reference manager in hiring competent staff and providing appropriate training and support for online services at the reference desk. In order for these services to be accepted and implemented successfully, the staff must be involved in the planning stages and assigned duties that complement their skills and interests.

On the evening of 10 March, Michael K. Buckland, assistant vice president for library plans and policy, University of California System, presented the Samuel Lazerow Memorial Lecture, with Steve Edwards, dean of faculties, Florida State University, presiding. The topic of this year's annual lecture was "The Vanishing Card Catalog." Buckland offered observations of the consequences of the shift from libraries that collect paper and microforms to contemporary libraries offering collections of paper, microforms, and machine readable information. After comparing and contrasting the functions of bibliographers and catalogers, he noted that they must now purchase services which were once a part of the library.

The conference concluded on the morning of 11 March, with the Seventh General Session. Lorraine D. Summers, assistant state librarian, State of Florida, presided and introduced the first speaker, Richard Boss, consultant, Information Systems Consultants, Inc. He provided a review and status report on "Current Uses of Automated Systems," noting that one cannot talk about current use without also including future uses. He pointed out that eighty percent of average library users are not concerned with the holdings, only with the availability of materials. As automated systems cease to be tools of library staff and become tools of the patrons, we will enhance the "bibliographic happiness" of our clients. He also discussed computer interfacing, standards, limitations of CD ROM, and expert systems.

The final speaker of the conference was Wayne A. Wiegand, associate professor, School of Library and Information Science, University of Wisconsin-Madison. Asked to address the human factor, Wiegand expounded on "People and Technology: A Delicate Balance." His introduction to this subject related that humans have the unique capability of selecting only those bits of information which they find useful, and that information without knowledge has no value. Today's sophisticated information retrieval systems should allow access to the information "wanted" and should not be restricted to that which is "needed."

V. LONNIE LAWSON
Ward Edwards Library
Central Missouri State University
Warrensburg, Missouri

BETH M. PASKOFF
School of Library and Information Science
Louisiana State University
Baton Rouge, Louisiana

ALPHONSE F. TREZZA
Professor
School of Library and Information Studies
Florida State University

Acknowledgments

Special thanks must go to Dean F. William Summers and the faculty and students of Florida State University School of Library and Information Studies, who not only participated in the program but also gave support, encouragement, and advice; and to the State Library of Florida for providing through an LSCA Title I grant, funds to support the distribution of copies of the proceedings of the conference to public libraries in Florida. The conference chairperson sincerely recognizes and appreciates the close and constant support and understanding of Dr. Mary L. Pankowski, director, and the staff of the Center for Professional Development and Public Service at Florida State University.

Introduction: Libraries and Changing Technology

WILLIAM J. WELSH
Deputy Librarian of Congress
Library of Congress
Washington, D.C.

I am going to talk about the year 2000, and I want you to remember that it wasn't John Naisbitt who told you this--it was Bill Welsh. Now I want you to imagine your kitchen; you have *The Joy of Cooking* online. In your bathroom you can access one of the databases of the National Library of Medicine and you can, for example, have stomach pain diagnosed or tell if you have an ingrown toenail. In the shop, the repair manual for an electric spoon is online. In the car, as you approach home, you can punch a series of buttons, have food moved from the freezer to the microwave oven, and have the food ready when you get home. In your public library, if you can join with me and imagine there the white-haired individual who was recently president of ALA, Bill Summers--his sole job is directing a number of robots to do the cataloging.

Now some of those things are very real right at this moment. You can, in fact, approach the Rift Valley outside of Nairobi, Kenya, and encounter a Masai tribesman who has some ailment. You can send a doctor in with two mules and carry a portable receiver the size of a suitcase on those two mules. You open the receiver up and again access the database of the National Library of Medicine. I've seen those suitcases unfold and know that we can communicate in this manner.

The year 2000 is not far off, but the message I want to leave with you is that the library is still alive and well. Regardless of what you believe about the role of the personal computer, I don't think that it is going to solve all of our problems. I think that when you begin to pay for all of the services that are available, you realize that the place where data files that support information are going to be is in your library. So, you students out there, keep looking for a job.

In the past several weeks I have testified before committees of both the House and the Senate of the Congress on behalf of the first application of optical disc technology. I want to tell you the background of that story and how it will affect your library. In 1980 I participated in the dedication of the Center for Biomedical Communications at the National Institutes of Health. Bill Baker, then chairman of the board at Bell Telephone Laboratories and a friend of mine, spoke to me at the dedication and suggested I stop what I was concentrating on in preservation and look at a new technology using optical discs, which he thought had great application for libraries. I checked with the chief scientists a Fairchild Corporation and at IBM to see if they had anything on the drawing board comparable to this technology; they did not, so I proceeded. The first thing I did was set up three committees in the Library of Congress. The first was a committee of technical experts; their job was to design a set of specifications for this technology, to apply it to library problems. The second committee served as a subcommittee of our Preservation Committee. I wanted them to see what forms and types of materials we should use in a three-year experiment using optical disc technology. The third committee was a "think committee." I don't like surprises; their job was to tell me what the future held for this technology. The first committee in fact did its business, wrote specifications, and made an award for three projects. The first project made use of a compact disc, such as you see here [disc shown to audience]. This disc has been produced by the Library of Congress; the hardware to use it is available off the shelf. The next application we made of that particular technology was to put music on it. We completed an experiment with this that proved that it works very well. You can put an hour of the finest quality sound imaginable on such a disc. Now we just have to adjust to this technology. Before this type of recording was available you could only record to the limits of the available technology. There are no limits to the range on this disc. You can record and experience the full range of highs and lows, more than was previously possible on a recording. This serves then as an example of either the analog or digital disc; we decided to produce both.

You can see by the reflection on the disc that this is laser produced and laser read. There are great advantages to this. The CD and the analog disc both represent what we call "shelf hardware." In other words, you can go to the store and get whatever you need in components to use the disc. The digital disc was not such a piece of "shelf hardware." The digital disc was created specifically for LC. As a result of this work a company named Integrated Automation produced the first jukebox for use with the digital discs. It looks something like the jukebox that older people around here might recognize, and handles 100 discs at one time. We originally launched a three-year experimental program utilizing optical discs. The program has been extended one year.

After we began the program we soon became aware that probably the greatest challenge we were going to face in this technology had to do with the copyright question. I appointed a committee of publishers and librarians to develop guidelines for handling this technology. They did that. They have now published their work and we are very pleased with the results.

We now have terminals installed so that the public can come in and access some of our collections either in the analog or the digital form. There are major differences between the analog and the digital discs. The analog is used to record only our nonprint material and the digital our print material. There is another fundamental difference. The analog disc system consists of a couple of discrete pieces of hardware, which are wired together at one's desk. You have to be right there to access the information. To access the information on the digital disc, however, you hardwire it, so the information can be stored in a separate location. We currently have eight terminals in the library from which to access the digital discs. So you, as a member of the public, can come in now and access the information we have in the system. Imagine, if you will, what this means to you. If you come to the library of Congress or any other library and want to find out what we have on the second battled of Manassas, for example, you have to go to our print collection, our photography collection, our music collection, our book collection, etc. Almost every collection we have includes some material on that particular subject. You have to move around from collection to collection. With this optical disc technology, that is not the case. You come in and sit down before a terminal that looks like an OCLC terminal. When you get the bibliographic information that you want, you call up the text. If you want a copy of the text that is available on the screen, you can ask for a printout. You never have to leave that particular location--all the data that you want are there.

The most important advantage of this technology is that is saves space. A library, unlike any other institution that I know about, continues to grow: we add new materials every year. There is a story about this particular problem. A number of years ago there was a great fire in a very large library. There are two schools of thought about that fire. One group of people thinks that we lost a lot of our cultural heritage in the fire and, of course, were saddened by this. Another group was relieved because, it after all had it not been for that fire, every square inch of Egypt would now be occupied by the old Alexandria Library. An exaggeration? Perhaps not. We add to our collections at the Library of Congress at the rate of 6,000 pieces per day. In 1980 we moved into our new building. We're now looking at the idea of a fourth library building-not necessarily a new structure, but the questioned how we are going to handle the growth. We have been growing at the rate of 44,000 square feet a year. The size of our staff has stabilized, but our collections continue to grow. How are we going to meet this challenge? Right here is one way of doing it. You can store the information remotely on optical disc and hardwire access to it from some other location. We have an annex in Landover, Maryland. We could readily move the optical disc jukebox out there and access the system from there.

The compaction of the analog disc allows you to store 54,000 images of each disc. On a single digital disc you can store several hundred books. You spoke, Dr. Sliger [FSU president], about items being in the bindery. With this technology there are no longer items away in the bindery. Once you put material on the disc, the information is there and the not-on-shelf problem disappears. In the present scheme of things, when someone else is using the item you want, you cannot also have access to it. In the optical disc system, you put a buffer system in so that any number of people can access the same information at the same time. Also, you have random accessibility. Unlike microfilm, if you index the information before putting it on the disc, you don't have to run through the whole reel. You can access in random fashion that which is of interest to you.

The discs can also be used to better preserve materials by enhancing the images. You can take some old sheet music, make copies of it through the scanning device, and the copies come out looking better than the original. So there are all sorts of possibilities for this format.

We still do not know how long a disc is going to last. We recently installed some ovens in the laboratory of the Library of Congress, and are testing the discs to see how much heat they will stand.

There are all sorts of challenges, as well. How do you load the disc? Conventionally in the Current Periodical Reading Room we wait until we assemble a number of issues of a title, usually on a yearly basis, and then bind them together. In order to take full advantage of the optical disc technology, you ought to scan an item as soon as the item comes into the library. But perhaps you might reload the items at the end of the year in order to have them in logical order. Imagine such a change in the way libraries are organized. The special reading rooms we now have in most large libraries won't be necessary in the future.

There is also the question of who will distribute the discs. the guidelines allow for the private sector to take care of their share of the market. What about classification? When you get information loaded on to a disc, you don't need LC or Dewey to locate the information on the shelves because it is going to be in this form. So

I think what we need to do in library schools is to find more effective uses for the Library of Congress classification system in retrieval. As far as the aspect of repackaging is concerned, you can put the information in any form possible, as we do in bibliographies new, but the number of packages is not limited as it is now.

We still have the issue of "fee versus free." What we are going to charge for becomes a very serious problem. My own view of this is that basic services must be free. At the same time, we ought to charge for extended services. It seems to me that, when the Xerox 914 came into being, we immediately decided to go the route of charging for copying. This is the way we can do it for this technology as well, as long as we have the right to scan information, bring it up on the screen, browse on the screen, and pay only for the printing costs. I think we can solve the perplexing problems with which we are faced. I think this technology is going to have a very, very serious impact upon the way we do business.

One of the matters I testified to in the past several weeks before Congress was the application of this technology to the work of our Congressional Research Service. We are going to try to put the contents of 3,000 currently used journals on optical disc, and have terminals in congressional offices so that office or committee staff can actually sit down before a terminal and have instant access to the documents themselves. This technology is not anything "blue sky." I know that we can do this now; we have already demonstrated it.

I recently visited Colorado State University. The people there were talking about constructing a library building for their engineering school. I asked them how many journals they need. The figure I was given was very modest, and I asked why build a building to house those journals. Why not put them on optical disc and give to every one of the faculty the contents of those journals via optical disc terminals on the desks? This may seem quite a dramatic change. It's going to take some time for all of the input into the databases. But look how fast we've come in bibliographic control. We now know pretty much what is available throughout this great country of ours.

There is one other item of interest some of you may have heard about: our project for the deacidification of books using diethyl zinc (DEZ). To say I've been annoyed with *Library Journal's Hotline* would be the understatement of my entire life. I think there is absolutely no excuse for the hostility that the journal has displayed in this matter. There have been problems with the project, and I want to tell you about them; I'll try to do it briefly. A number of years ago, in the 1970s, we had a staff of chemists who came up with a process for the elimination of acid from book material using diethyl zinc and a pressure cooker. A household pressure cooker, which would hold four books, was originally used. Four books were put in the cooker, the moisture was drawn out by a vacuum, and diethyl zinc vapor was pumped in. When the process was completed and we removed the books, we realized that we had eliminated the acid that was in those four books, even though the books were closed in the chamber. Well, the group of four books was obviously not large enough to demonstrate the validity of the process. So we went to the General Electric Space Center at Valley Forge and used one of their small vacuum chambers. We tested the process again and found that it still worked. Then we needed the project scaled up, so we went to NASA's Goddard Space Flight Center outside of Washington. The staff there agreed to modify one of their big chambers, a chamber that is 8 1/2 feet in diameter and 15 feet in length. They modified the vacuum chamber, took off some of the solar energy equipment that they were using on it, and we loaded 5,000 books into it and tried the process again. This first experiment did not work fully. We removed 640 pounds of water in the process. When we opened the doors some five days later, we found that the books on the bottom had been neutralized, but not the books on the top. So we had to change the venting for the diethyl zinc vapor, we changed the pumping, and we discovered it worked. Then we ran a whole series of smaller tests, under contract with NASA. We decided then that we needed to build a pilot plant, a smaller facility to test some of the other forms of material like manuscripts, prints, and photographs.

The day before we ran the first test at the facility, I was so pleased with the results to date that I took our top staff to look at the plant itself. All off this was done with NASA staff, so the plant was constructed with no special equipment, but with stuff that they had available such as vacuum pumps. The following day they had decided to run through a test without any books in the chamber. As it was determined later, there were several mechanical failures. The diethyl zinc was shipped in a liquid form from Houston, Texas. To use it you had to distill it and put it in a vapor state so that it could be piped into the chamber. One of the mechanical failures was that the heater that keeps the temperature constant in the pipes feeding the chamber--so that the DEZ stays in vapor--was improperly plugged in. The diethyl zinc thus came into the chamber in liquid form and gathered at the bottom. The next step is something called passivation, when they introduce water to cleanse the chamber. When the water mixed with the DEZ in liquid form, it raised the temperature inside the chamber and the door opened. When the DEZ came in contact with the air, there was one heck of a fire, at about 8,000 degrees. The fire was put out in a matter of seconds because of a built-in suppression system. There was a three-month investigation of this incident. After the investigation was completed they decided that they knew what went wrong. Then, to find out how much diethyl zinc was still in the system, they began to open the system and bleed it, valve by valve. Another failure occurred. Incidentally, in the first failure there should have been a warning that the temperature in the chamber had risen. That warning device did not function either, which means that there were two controls that did not operate properly. In the process of bleeding the system, there was another fire. This time there was a small explosion and the walls of the building moved out ever so slightly, about a foot. The tragedy at Cape Canaveral occurred between the first mishap and the second so NASA was very conscious of bad publicity, as were we. Up to that time there had been a lot of damage, but nobody had been hurt and no materials had been lost. They decided that they had to relieve the pressure in the system, but what they didn't know was that instead of having several pounds of DEZ in the system, there was a great quantity inside. Again they didn't know this because of the failure of a part to function properly. They called me one morning, and I'll never forget this as long as I live, and said that they were going to bring in the Army and attach what they called shaped charges. The charge is something that looks like a piece of rope. They wrap it around the pipe where they want to separate the pipe and release the pressure. They are so skillful with this that they could take the stem off of your watch. But it didn't sound to me as if this was the right approach. I volunteered to go out with an infrared camera and identify where the pressure was. This process was used before and I was confident that they could do this. But they decided that because of the incident at the Cape they wanted to get on with it as quickly as possible. Well, there was an explosion and a fire. They decided not to challenge the fire, so it burned for about an hour. We got all of the bad publicity about this.

I think that we have learned a great deal from all of this at the library, although it was very painful for us. We have now signed a contract with Texas Alkyls, a firm in Houston, Texas, to build a new test facility for us. In the meantime, Congress gave us 11.5 million dollars and we put out bids for the construction of the big facility at Fort Detrick. We decided not to award the bid until we have more answers to the problems. Congress has now assigned the Office of Technology Assessment the responsibility for looking at what we have done and making sure that we haven't made any mistakes. The one critical mistake that was made was our assumption that NASA had all the answers. What we didn't realize was that NASA didn't have the chemical processing staff to do this work, nor do we. In going to Texas Alkyls, a firm that works with chemicals every day of the week, we are confident that they will know what to do. By September the test plant there will be completed and we will be able to run the tests and get back in the right direction.

The greatest problem we face as librarians is that the destruction of the printed word is caused not by fire, but by the acid that is contained in the paper itself. Ninety-seven percent of our book materials contain acid. Over three million of them are embrittled, so that if you try to bend the page more than three times, it breaks. Approximately 77,000 titles a year in the Library of Congress's collections move from the seriously acidic state to the brittle state. We have been doing microfilming for 14 years. This is the only technology that is readily available right now to solve the embrittled book problem. We have spent $16 million and we've filmed fewer than 400,000 titles out of the three million that we have in the brittle state. Even though we have a very productive microfilming program, that is not enough to do even one half of the volumes that are becoming brittle each year. So we've got a major problem and you have a major problem as well. All libraries have this problem.

The Commission on Preservation and Access is going to address this matter. We had hearings on Tuesday, 3 March, before the Subcommittee on Postsecondary Education in the House of Representatives. We hope to get some money distributed throughout the country. We know exactly how many volumes are in the state of deterioration about which we have to do something. But we also have to deal with incoming materials. If we don't, then we are going to continue to build the major problem. So the diethyl zinc system gives us our solution to treat all the incoming materials and to try to treat all the stuff that is on the shelves that has not as yet become brittle. We will use optical disc technology for serial publications because I think that is the perfect answer for problems associated with using and preserving that material.

I have two diagrams here that will illustrate my point. What is shown here are four pages from a journal and a two-millimeter pinhead. Those four pages fit in the space of that pinhead on the optical disc. That addresses the problem of space. Here are some other examples. All of the books shown in that area can be held on that number of optical discs. All of the contents of twenty to thirty years of *Time* magazine can be stored on those twelve discs. This is one of the areas where I believe that we can make enormous strides.

But we need all of the solutions known to us. For the brittle books problem, we need to deal with the incoming materials because most of us still want to preserve our books in their original format. We want to use optical disc technology on things like newspapers and serials, where the content is more important than the format. We will have to use cold storage for preservation of some of the color materials we have. We will continue to investigate all other forms of preservation and service. When an item comes into the library we must look at it from the preservation point of view and continue from there. We have got to look at acquisitions, cataloging, service, and preservation issues and make some decisions that reflect what it is we are going to save. I don't think that we can save it all.

Some years ago I had lunch with Mortimer Adler. I asked him what he thought we should save in the Library of Congress. He said that that was a pretty difficult question; why don't we just say what we were going to throw away. I said, "okay, what about Zane Grey novels? How do you feel about *The Bobbsey Twins and the Houseboat*? How do you feel about the Sears Roebuck catalog?" He asked why would anyone want to keep the Sears Roebuck catalog, and I said because under a single cover you have a great record of our culture. But there are millions of examples like that. In our case, we have 84 million items in the collection. We've got to decide if we are going to keep all 35 million manuscripts in the original format. We can't do it. Who is going to make the decision? It's a question that won't wait; it's here with us now.

What do you have in Florida that represents a unique collection in the whole country? We should have the dean of a library school give his students the challenge of coming up with a list of a half dozen collections that represent something unique in the state of Florida, and we should worry about preserving those materials. I understand that there is a lady here from Iceland, a student. She may be surprised to know that the greatest collection of Icelandic materials exists not in Iceland, but at Cornell University. Cornell acquired those materials when it had a great study program on that country. They no longer have the great interest in that area of study; what will happen to that great collection? That question is duplicated over and over again. The Library of Congress has a great collection of early Russian newspapers. Should we keep that as our first priority because it is such a priceless collection? We have preserved it in its original format. There are certain things that ought to be kept in the original format. For example, we ought to keep the *New York Times* in original format to show the children of our next generation what it looked like to have this paper.

We've got some hard decisions to make, and I don't think we're getting stimulated enough to meet the challenge. We've got to do it together. Money is not going to be available for all we need to do. We will have to work with the technology, and with the idea that our role is one of service. We are not saving things just for the sake of preservation, but for the service we can provide. Let's get on with it.

PART 1
Centralized and Distributed Databases: Is the Balance Tilting?

National Databases and Linkages

M. E. L. JACOB
Vice President, Library Planning
Online Computer Library Center (OCLC)
Dublin, Ohio

Last year at the conference on multitype library networks I spoke about the future of national networks and reiterated my belief that they did indeed have a future.[1] But in that future they would probably become very different organizations from what they are now, providing a broad variety of new services to an enlarged group of users, including not only library staffs and patrons, but also other information providers such as publishers, faculties, students, professionsals, and even general citizens. This paper will focus more closely on what some of the nearterm changes may be, how they will affect libraries, and some of the issues we will have to resolve to make these new types of linkages work.

What kinds of linkages presently exist and how do they work? Linkages mean many things to many people, but primarily of interest to most libraries is the ability to move data from one site to another and be able to perform a variety of functions on that data. Linkages may be contractual via some medium such as tape, CDROM, floppy disk, or telecommunication. Currently most national networks use all of these.

Linkages may also be between different types of organizations. They may link a terminal in a library to a network via dedicated or dial-up as in figure 1; a local network-to-network as in figure 2; a network-to-LC or a network-to-another-network as in figure 3. These linkages can become quite complex with all types of relationships occurring at once.

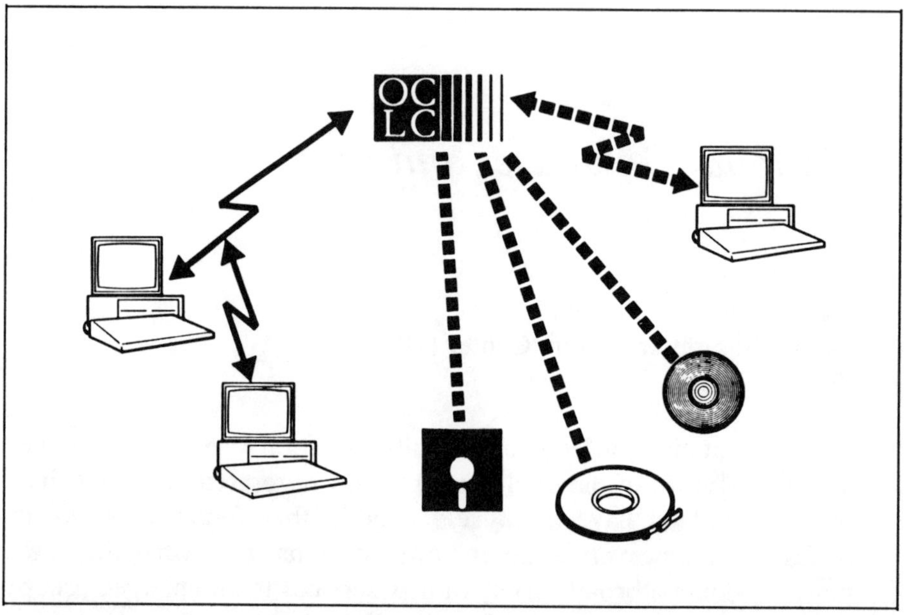

Figure 1

These linkages may be accomplished in a number of different ways. They may employ VANs, gateways, or LSP. VANs are value-added networks such as Tymnet and Telenet that are used for dial access. Telenet has established an X.25 packet network that creates virtual circuits that behave much like dedicated line access with auto logon capabilities, micro computers or workstations, and appropriate software. With such features the difference in function between dial access and dedicated terminals blurs.

Gateways provide a means of using one telecommunication system to reach another computer system. In one sense VANs provide gateways. Usually, however, gateways are used for systems like Mead's access to Dialog, OCLC Link with acces to Wilsonline, VuText, and Dialog, and Dialog access to the Official Airline Guide which is accessible to Dialog users, but maintained by the OAG on a separate computer system. Intelligent gateways may, in fact, not only access a system, but translate user queries into commands acceptable to the host system. Such gateways must be continually updated to ensure new commands and responses are available on all the host systems and can be used, or at the least not cause the system to fail.

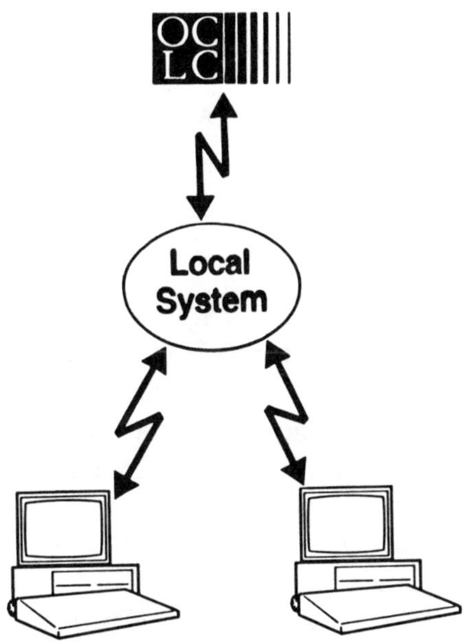

Figure 2

Figure 3

The Linked Systems Protocols of the Linked Systems Project (LSP) are similar to an intelligent gateway, but require all participating systems to agree on what commands and messages they will exchange and how they are formatted. LSP is based on the International Standards Organization Open System Interconnection Model. This model is defined in seven layers and identifies functions appropriate to each. X.25 corresponds to the bottom three layers (see figure 4). LSP focuses primarily on the top layer, the applications layer using standardized protocols for the lower layers.[2] Currently LSP is being used by OCLC and LC and RLIN and LC for LC distribution of authority data. Copies of LC authority records are pulled daily and used to update files at RLIN and OCLC. Work is currently underway to modify LSP protocols for the exchange of bibliographic records.

ISO – OSI REFERENCE MODEL

Layer	Type	LSP
7	Applications	Authorities
6	Presentation	(Dummy)
5	Session	(Draft ISO)
4	Transport	(Draft ISO)
3	Network	X.25
2	Link	↓
1	Physical	

Figure 4

Among some of the issues relating to linking are:

- Data Content
- Telecommunication
- Quality of Service
- Staff Skills
- Economics

Data Format and Content

Current networks and most libraries are committed to the use of the MARC format for the exchange of data. The definition and maintenance of these formats are the responsibility of the Library of Congress and MARBI. It is also influenced by international agreements, however, particularly those between the ABBACUS libraries: The national libraries of Australia, Canada, and the United Kingdom, and the Library of Congress. Much of the present US MARC format is LC-centric and contains some fields restricted to LC internal use.

Data content depends on what catalog rules, classification system, and subject approach are used. Most US national networks follow LC practice but may also accommodate other forms such as OCLC does for the NLM classification, and subject headings and for Precis for UK MARC. Data content may become more of an issue as other organizations such as publishers begin to supply bibliographic records or full text data.

Important in relation to format and content is the ability of all linked systems to implement systems changes at the same time or in close agreement. Otherwise one or another system may be unable to send, receive, or process data from others. A recent problem experienced by U.S. networks was a unilateral change made by the US ISBN agency in the format of the ISBN without proper notification to other publishers, LC, or the networks.

Telecommunication

Once local or regional networks are created they may affect the ability of a service provider to isolate and correct problems, may reduce costs for some but raise costs for others, and provide different levels and quality of service to users even in the same geographic region. Some universitites are developing their own campus-wide system, while some states are developing systems for state and public agencies, but may exclude private or for-profit bodies.

Quality of service may be highly variable. Currently OCLC users can expect certain levels of performance for the OCLC system in repsonse time and messages. As more local systems try to become the primary interface for their users it changes what the user sees on the local terminal affecting what is displayed and how. It may also affect what error messages are returned. This presents major challenges to both OCLC and local systems designers in relation to coordinating documentation and training. Response on a terminal connected directly to OCLC is likely to be very different from a terminal on a local system when that system is then connected to OCLC. Another layer of software and hardware must be passed through in order to communicate with the user. A local system may not support all the features available on OCLC. If not, will it allow the user to communicate and receive OCLC commands and messages, in essence functioning as a gateway? If the local system has problems, how will they be resolved and who will notify the user?

System Enhancement

In addition to data and content format changes, there can also be changes in screen display, commnads, and error messages or responses. Depending on how the system interface is defined, change by one system in any of these could mean another system would be unable to process data, commands, or messages. Synchronizing such changes is essential if linked systems are to continue to communicate. This may result in forcing one or the other to hold off on introducing new features until all partners can implement code or it may mean some features will only be available to certain users. This presents major problems for documentation and training. OCLC has been wrestling with this issue in regard to how different terminals with different cursors, cursor control, and keyboards will be used on its new system and how to represent this in OCLC documentation.

Staff Skills

As we develop more complex systems and linkages it will also mean we will need more knowledgeable staff to operate them. Not only will programmers, data administrators, and computer operators be needed, but so will telecommunications experts. We can contract with third party agencies for some services, but we cannot rely on turnkey vendors, service agencies, or consultants to solve all our operating problems. Nor can we afford the costs of doing so.

Economics

Our libraries exist in an increasingly complex world. We have to choose intelligently between various options and seek maximum benefit with the least penalties. Cost is one aspect. Cost includes telecommunication and access charges, staff, equipment or network maintenance, software enchancement and maintenance, backup and recovery procedures, system growth, and charges for data or services.

In such a world it is easy either to become discouraged by its complexity or to pay more than we should just to continue present activities.

The Future

The future will be chaotic with all types of linkages. We will not have a national network that is hierarchical, is operated by one system, or is a fully distributed system. Rather we will have overlapping spheres of influence and we will have local systems and clusters, university systems, state systems, and national data bases (figure 5). Functions will change with gateways becoming increasingly important for all systems. Will these systems provide improved cost-effective access? Only time will tell, but so too will our efforts to create and shape such linkages.

Our challenge is to preserve the best of our present system, while adding new functions and changing our relationships and what we require of these systems. Are there risks? Yes, but we build the future we want as long as we continue to educate ourselves and the system providers about the possibilities and our needs.

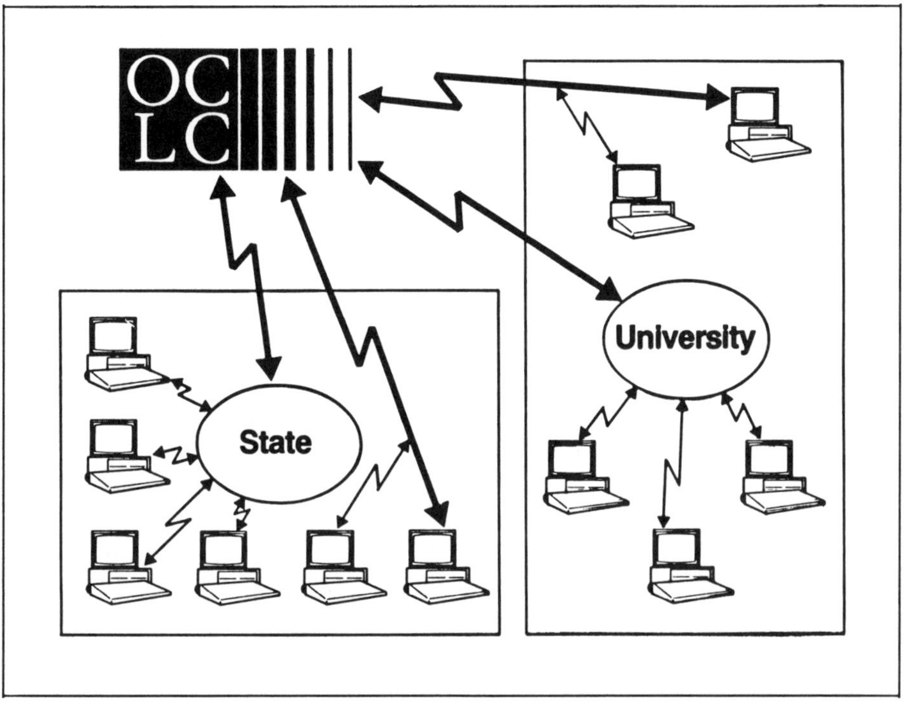

Figure 5

Notes

1. M. E. L. Jacob, "Changing Roles: National Networks and Future" in *Not Alone . . . But Together: A Conference on Multitype Library Cooperation*, ed. Alphonse F. Trezza (Tallahassee: Florida State University, 1987).

2. Howard Turtle, "The Open Systems Interconnection (OSI) Reference Model," in *Telecommincations Networks Issues and Trends*, ed. M. E. L. Jacob (White Plains, N.Y.: Knowledge Industries, 1986).

Local Systems and Distributed Processing

EMILY GALLUP FAYEN
Assistant Director of Libraries for Systems
University of Pennsylvania
Philadelphia, Pennsylvania

Library systems are entering a new era, one in which individual libraries can have their own systems working in partnership with other libraries or library systems. In the early days of library automation only a few large institutions could afford to have computer-based systems. Institutions such as NASA, the National Library of Medicine, the Library of Congress, some large universities, and IBM itself plus a few other large corporations were the only ones who could afford the high cost of building and maintaining the computer systems that were needed. At the same time, the costs of cataloging, catalog card production, and filing continued to climb. Recognizing a critical need and responding to the realities of the time, OCLC began to offer time-shared services to libraries. They offered shared cataloging, card production facilities, acquisitions, and serials support. OCLC's success led others to enter the field. The Research Libraries Group, the Washington Library Network, UTLAS, and a host of regional network support groups (NELINET, PALINET, SOLINET, AMIGOS, and so forth) were formed. These groups all depended on the critical need for computer support services among libraries and the economics of the time when the cost of owning a computer powerful enough to provide these services made it prohibitively expensive for most libraries. This arrangement led to coining of the term "bibliographic utility" and these large providers of bibliographic data were looked on as services similar to the electric company.

By 1975, the bibliographic utility was a fact of life and libraries all over the country were busily building machine-readable databases corresponding to their library holdings. At the same time, a need for local systems support was developing. Not only was cataloging data required but libraries needed automated circulation systems to support burgeoning user demands and they dreamed of the online integrated library system which would solve all their operating problems.

Still later, as the needs of technical processing began to be met by local systems, database services were made available to the public by means of the online public catalog, or OPAC as it is often called. These machine-readable catalogs have changed forever how we and our users think about the library. No longer is the library solely a quiet repository for books; in addition it has become the focal point for research and scholarly study of all kinds.

Even more recently, there has been a dramatic shift in the economics of library computing. The cost of computer processing and online data storage continue to fall dramatically while the cost of telecommunications continues to rise. At the same time, computer processing power for the dollar, or bang for the buck, is also increasing rapidly. Consequently, it is now economically feasible for many libraries to install local systems. Once again, we have seen a host of library systems vendors rush in with new products to meet this need. Almost any size library can now find appropriate software and hardware to support a local system at a price the library can afford. As a result, many libraries are installing local systems, some of which are still linked to one or more vendors of cataloging data such as OCLC or FAXON. Others are beginning to challenge the economic feasibility of this way of doing things and are developing local systems which are much more nearly self-sufficient. The impact of this shift is only now being recognized, and its full effects are not yet known. However, the movement to local systems raises some economic and theoretical questions which need to be answered before we inadvertently destroy something of inestimable value in the desperate need to save money in the short run.

These local library systems could be viewed as "stand-alone library support systems." Because they almost always have links of some kind with another system or library, however, they are usually characterized as providing "distributed processing." Distributed processing is a somewhat over-used term that unfortunately is used in two quite different senses in this context.

The Bibliographic Utilities Model

Bibliographic utilities are distributed processing systems in which part of the processing is performed locally using an intelligent workstation. The system has a physically unified database, and some of the data processing takes place centrally, as well as at the workstation. Thus, the database is *centralized*, while the processing (at least some of it) is *decentralized* or distributed.

The big advantage to this approach is that all users have access to the entire data base. The bibliographic utility can be used as a source of records for local modules such as serials receipt control or acquisitions as well as a source of information for cataloging. The data may also be shared with other bibliographic utilities or systems via a common protocol such as the Linked Systems Protocol (LSP). This procedure will allow both authority and bibliographic data to be shared among various systems.

The disadvantages of this approach are that the telecommunications costs are high and seem destined to go higher. Further, it can be extremely costly to maintain both a local database and the data in the bibliographic utility.

The Local Systems Model

An alternative approach is the Local Systems Model, one in which each library has its own local automated integrated library system. Although the implementation of such a system will vary tremendously from library to library, these systems generally consist of the following modules or subsystems:

- Catalog record creation and maintenance
- Full MARC record support for import and export
- Authority control
- Acquisitions
- Serials receipt
- Circulation
- Online Public Access Catalog
- Interlibrary Loan et al.

The first three functions are required if a library wants to provide for itself some of the functions of the bibliographic utility. With these three modules or subsystems in place, the library can perform original cataloging, conduct retrospective conversion projects, or use cataloging data from other sources such as CDROM files of LC records or the LC MARC tapes themselves.

Many libraries find this approach attractive because it may provide the same end result at lower overall cost. However, it may also be extremely dangerous because it can lead to the gradual erosion of the strong central data base that is the heart of the bibliographic utilities model. It is possible to envision a scenario in which in just a short time, the large, integrated bibliographic utility database simply ceases to exist and is replaced by a collection of distributed databases and systems.

This shift could seriously weaken Interlibrary Loan and could make it much more difficult and costly to do retrospective conversion and other projects which depend on a strong central database.

Is It Inevitable?

Economic pressures seem to be the major force moving libraries to local systems. Many libraries have installed local systems in order to provide online catalogs and automated circulation services for their patrons. Faced with the high cost of continuing to provide these services, libraries are looking for other ways to use the equipment, software, and support staff to reduce other library costs. Moving certain functions from a bibliographic utility to the local system has great appeal. Such a move immediately leads to lower telecommunication costs and perhaps reduced out-of-pocket costs for the library. In addition, many institutions welcome such a move because of the greater autonomy and independence it gives them.

The key issue here, however, is how to move with this trend without losing the strong central databases we have. We need to preserve a functional equivalence, while changing the operating environment as needed.

Remedies Proposed

Two possible approaches to solving this problem are development of a bidirectional Linked Systems Protocol and a broadcast search capability. Enhancement of the Linked System Protocol with a two-way link would enable libraries with local systems to send bibliographic records to their respective bibliographic utilities so that the central database would remain a resource for all users. If this protocol could be implemented so that libraries would not have to pay too much to send records back to the host system, all would be encouraged to participate. Perhaps libraries could be given a credit (much as they are now) for original records that are contributed to the central database.

If this approach does not work and in a few years, the large bibliographic utility of today is replaced by several local systems, development of a broadcast query capability might allow all the libraries to share each others data files. Imagine, for example, sending an Interlibrary Loan request to 20 libraries simultaneously in hopes of locating a copy of the desired work rather than looking for the item in a bibliographic utility database. As far as the requesting library and the patron, the result is exactly the same, but in reality, there is no shared database. Instead, there is a "virtual" database that is physically distributed among several library systems. Thus, we have a catalog database that is logically one, but is physically distributed.

The terminal becomes a sort of window on the world where a patron or staff member can search the collection of a library anywhere it happens to be. Once located, the next step is to obtain a copy of the item for the requester. As libraries cope with declining budgets and heightened expectations, new delivery services may be needed. The challenge is to take advantage of new technology to allow libraries to operate as cost effectively as possible without destroying a national resource of inestimable value.

Peaceful Coexistence

JOAN S. SEGAL
Executive Director
Association of College and Research Libraries
Chicago, Illinois

Considering that we are dealing in this conference with an area where change is occurring at a dizzying pace, I find the title of this session and of my paper comfortingly familiar. In fact, sometimes you can have the pleasant surprise of finding that, whereas you thought you were in unfamiliar territory, the terrain suddenly becomes recognizable. I'll give you an example.

My mother and dad retired to Florida a few years ago; they live in Tamarac, near Fort Lauderdale. They like to get around the state exploring and learning the new territory. One day they found themselves in a place with one of those unfamiliar Seminole(?) names, Kissimmee. They didn't know how to pronounce it, and neither did their companions, another retired couple. So they decided to ask the waitress.

"Excuse me," said my dad, "but could you please tell us the name of this place, and would you say it *real* slow, so we can get it right?"

And the waitress said, "BUR-GER KING."

Now in relation to the topic we are considering today, the centralized and decentralized aspects of networking, I find that, although I may have thought I was in a strange land, the parameters defined by the titles are extremely familiar. The title, "Centralized and Distributed Databases: Is the Balance Tilting?" sets the tone. It implies that there is supposed to be some kind of balance between centralized and distributed networking and that the greater weight had been on one side or the other and may now be changing, so that the scale will reveal by its tilt that there is more of a counterweight on the other side.

In fact, the assumption has been made in may quarters that there has been too great a weight on centralized databases and networks and that decentralization is necessary to replace formerly centralized sources of information with locally constructed and maintained files. A sense of intrigue plays around the periphery of these matters, and is intermingled with a sense of the ultimate victory of the little guy against the big bad forces of centralization. "Have we brought national networks to their knees?" is another way to phrase the title question.

But just as familiar as the title is the cast of characters on this panel. Mary Ellen Jacob has been a spokesperson for OCLC, national databases, and linking for many years. She can be counted on to present fairly the argument for maintaining such databases and linkages. Emily Gallup Fayen has been identified closely with Dartmouth's efforts to build it online catalog, including a number of innovative assays at local database building and maintenance. And I have a reputation for smoothing; for rejecting polarization of positions; and, perhaps excessively, for looking for ways to promote "peaceful coexistence" in potentially troublesome situations, often by redefining those situations.

Thus, the conference planners have set up for you a classical panel, the epitome of what such as session should be. And I shall play my part, although I may modify the "givens" just a little bit in doing so.

What Are Centralization and Decentralization?

The *Glossary for Library Networking*, prepared by the Network Development Office at the Library of Congress, defines a centralized (computer) network as a configuration in which one computer or a group of centrally located computers provides computer power and maintains control of application-level programs and telecommunications; and centralized processing as computer processing in which one computer or a group of centrally located computers provides power and maintains network control. A decentralized (computer) network has computing power and/or control functions distributed over several network nodes. Distributed databases are logically interconnected databases (or portions of a database, such as the indices) that reside in separate physical locations in a network. A distributed network is a network design in which each node is connected to every other node either directly or through an intermediate node. In this commonly shared set of definitions, the difference between distributed and decentralized networks or processing does not exist; the terms are used synonymously.

Technologically speaking, networks are simply a way of connecting people, institutions, and/or equipment.[1] Some of the most common network configurations are: the ring, the star, and the tree. Simple drawings of these are helpful in envisioning the way messages are passed along the network.

In the ring, each node is connected to the previous and next node. Each node may initiate, receive, or send on any message. There is no centralized control, which sometimes gives rise to congestion in the system, or to a garbling of messages. My favorite example of a ring communication system is the children's game of "gossip," where one child begins by whispering a message to the next child, who in turn whispers it to the next child. The last child revealed what he or she heard; the message is almost always distorted, which is good for a laugh! But such distortion is not desirable in the real world. In library networking, an example of a ring network would be the round-robin interlibrary loan network, either using the mail or computers.

The star configuration has a central node, with spokes travelling out to each of the other nodes. All messages pass through the central node on the way to their final destination. This pattern is common among library networks; DIALOG and the bibliographic utilities are *essentially* star networks.

The tree, or hierarchical network, is one that is familiar to librarians. Messages flow up the hierarchy only as far as the lowest level at which they can be handled. An example is the Regional Medical Library network,[2] where interlibrary loans are filled at the lowest possible level, but move further "up" the hierarchy until the request can be filled.

An interesting aside to the networking configuration matter is some work in the field of human communication,[3] in which several networking patterns were compared for accuracy, speed of transmission, and satisfaction level. It was found that the star network, where one key person receives and forwards all messages, is most accurate and fastest, but provides least satisfaction for experimental subjects. A ring topology, where messages are passed around the circle without a central person, is slowest and least accurate, but most satisfying for the subjects. A hierarchical structure gives intermediate results.

What is misleading is that most networks are actually *mixed*. For instance, the Regional Medical Library Network, just described, includes a centralized database for NLM (National Library of Medicine) periodicals, but regional databases for the periodical holdings of the regional centers. The collection is distributed in medical libraries throughout the country, and decision-making and funding are mixed, depending on may factors. This kind of mixed configuration is most common. A database may be centralized, and access distributed. Governance may be distributed, but technical control centralized. Economic factors may need centralized handling, but the telecommunication system may be decentralized.

Finally, it should be realized that networks may appear to have one configuration, while actually having another. The concepts of virtuality and of transparency have been used to make network operations appear simple because of their elegant design. In a virtual system, a number of point-to-point circuits are connected through switching by communications computers, such that the circuit of data transfer appears to the user as a single physical transmission path.[4] Most commonly, a system where a user logs on only once and uses a common command language to view data that may reside on several external computers is referred to as "transparent."[5]

Two important issues concerning centralized networks are: 1) what is at the center of the network, and 2) what kind of control is exercised. At the center of the network may be one or more of the following: a database, a computer system, a telecommunications system, and/or a staff of people. Depending on the nature of this center, the network will have a different appearance and will be perceived differently. For instance, if some of these elements are at the center and others are distributed, the network may appear to be distributed, despite the fact that some of its most important elements are centralized.[6]

The nature of the control is also extremely important. A bulletin board system, for instance, is totally centralized in terms of telecommunication and the database and compute system. However, most such systems exercise no control over the content of the database (which has resulted in some catastrophes, where a "practical joker" enters a program that unsuspecting users install, only to find it has erased their entire files!)

On the other hand, there may be complete control. For instance, the Washington State Library not only owns and controls the WLN computer system and telecommunications system, but it provides all staffing for the network and exercises total control over the content of the database by a professional review of all records entered. There are many advantages of a central node for a network, but the question of who would coordinate and manage such a node in a nationwide network of libraries in the US was a major factor in the development of networking here, and we do not have such a monolithic, national network.[7]

Aspects of Database Work

Looking at the networking question from the point of view of a tilting balance forces us to think of a zero-sum game. That is, a game or situation where, if one side wins, the other side must lose. I think there is a great deal of this kind of thinking going on at the moment concerning centralization and decentralization, and concerning networks of different kinds. I would prefer to think of centralization, decentralization, linking, and integration as methods appropriate for different aspects of database work.

For instance, we can look at centralized library networks--both in a historical sense and in terms of today's needs-as the most effective method for much *database building.* The creation of the massive databases of OCLC, RLIN, and UTLAS was only possible through the cooperative efforts of major cataloging sources, such as the Library of Congress, and the thousands of libraries that contribute their cataloging to them. The sheer size of these databases makes it increasingly likely that a given item will be found; all but the largest research libraries find 95 percent of the items they wish to catalog on their host system.

Similarly, it can be argued that decentralization is the best mode for *database use*. The ability to format a database to be most helpful to the particular library's users and to design software aimed at a specific clientele, the capacity to include in the database exactly what the library's patrons need, the tailoring of a system to accommodate the host computer of a parent institution, such as a municipal government or a campus, or the freedom to experiment with new ideas on the system all call for a decentralized mode.

Linking is the networking mode of choice for *database sharing*. After years of hard work, the Linked Systems Project (LSP) is bearing fruit, with authorities data now being exchanged, and the promise of other data exchanges soon to come. While centralized networks already allow us to share data, inter-system linkages will broaden our ability to share with others. Not only effective at the level of RLIN, OCLC, and LC, the perfecting of the LSP will open the way to exchanges between decentralized systems in the future.

Toward an Integrated Library System

Rather than a "peaceful coexistence" between centralized and decentralized networks, I envision an *integrated* system within a library, where a variety of modes of networking are used to accomplish the database work of the library.

In such a system, databases are built and added to using centralized sources, such as OCLC, RLIN, and UTLAS. Databases are used for local purposes and, while they may be built on a set of common principles, they will each be different, tailored to the needs of the individual institution. Database sharing via linking and use of centralized networks will allow the library to enhance access to information for its users and for other resource sharing purposes. Local databases may integrate catalog and reference bibliographic data and nonbibliographic data from local, state, regional, and national sources, via centralized database access, local storage media such as CD ROM, linkages with other systems, and arrangements with local suppliers, such as university research centers.

Levels of Networking

To accomplish the goal of local library system integration, networks are needed at a variety of levels. These levels are also not to be considered as a zero-sum game. Despite Tom Ballard's claim that networks are merely larger units of service which distance the user form the source of information,[8] I believe they may more realistically be seen as agencies able to provide expert services to librarians that allow them to better serve their users. Some of the levels and the services that might be provided at each are:

National:

Large databases of bibliographic data for cataloging and acquisitions must be maintained and kept strong.

Large databases of bibliographic information for reference purposes must also be maintained and kept strong.

Large databases of holdings information for interlibrary loan and other resource sharing efforts must be kept current.

Telecommunication networks along which data may be transferred must be created and maintained; costs must be kept at a minimum through application of technological and political expertise.

Multistate Regional:

Large-scale wholesale access to the above must be provided.

Large-volume technical assistance is needed, which includes tape manipulation services, installation, consulting.

Training in technical systems is offered.

Telecommunications savings may be afforded through multiplexers, etc.

Contract and accounting services are handled by accessible staff members.

Statewide:

Assistance is offered with reference questions, collection development, and other functions, especially for small libraries.

Telecommunications networks may be supported by state government, helping in the linkage of several institutions within a state. State databases may be maintained, including statewide catalogs of library holdings, union lists of serials, college course curricula, economic development information.

Consortial:

Cooperative actions are geared toward the sharing of bibliographic and other data for online catalogs that include the collections and status of materials in a group of institutions.

Local:

Campus telecommunication systems link library to other parts of institution.

CD ROM may be used to store time-insensitive information.

Databases produced by local government, university research centers, private industry can be collected.

Online catalog of library holdings is available.

Conclusion

If changing technology is to provide an opportunity and a challenge, it will be because it forces us to re-examine some of our assumptions and allows us to take advantage of new ways of doing our work. And if that work is directed at the goal of providing access to information in all its forms to all people, then changing technology offers us the opportunity to provide better access and makes us question our thinking about the methods we have been using, such as networking.

We can see every change as a threat--to ourselves, to our libraries, to our society, or to some institution. To some extent, that is what underlies the "tilting balance" concept. But it is far more realistic, I believe, to greet change as a natural process and to seize the chance it gives us to improve our condition, our work, and our attitudes.

Peaceful coexistence between warring factions is better than war, perhaps. But a broader framework that accommodates all sides of a question may allow us the vision to escape the traps that such a stalemate portends. Here a consideration of Hegel's philosophy of the dialectic might be useful. Hegel asserted that all human activity could only be understood by examining its history and that there is a tendency in history to progress through several phases. The first phase tends to give way to another phase that is opposite to it, and still later, by a third phase, the is a resolution of the first two. This in fact, becomes the first phase of a new cycle. After Hegel (perhaps with Fichte), the terms *thesis*, *antithesis,* and *synthesis* were used to identify these three phases. The thesis and antithesis can be seen as two ends of a continuum. The synthesis encompasses the entire continuum and sees both thesis and antithesis as part of a whole.

So much for the formal theory. My piano teacher, Antonia Brico, used to refer to the three-week cycle. At the lesson in the first week, the teacher tells the student the tempo of the piece is too slow. The second week, the student will almost certainly play the piece too fast. It takes until the third week for the student to get the tempo right!

I would like to think of the history of networking as first having a period of building up a centralized database and network, followed by a period in which the technology has enabled institutions to build up more capacity at the local level. I hope these two will be replaced by a new awareness of the advantages of both centralization and decentralization and the need libraries have to use resources, capacities, and services at numerous levels to support their work and service.

Notes

1. Jerry Fitzgerald and Tom S. Eason, *Fundamentals of Data Communications* (New York: John Wiley & Sons, 1978).

2. Robert M. Braude, "National Networking--The Regional Medical library Model," *Resource Sharing and Information Networks* 1, no.3/4 (Spring/Summer 1984):107-24.

3. Gerald M. Goldhaber, *Organizational Communication* (Dubuque: William C. Brown Co., 1974).

4. U.S. Library of Congress, Network Development Office, *A Glossary for Library Networking* (Washington, D.C.: Library of Congress, 1978) Network Planning Paper no. 2.; Prepared by Dataflow Systems, Inc., for Network Development Office.

5. Cynthia J. Durance, Edwin J. Buchinski, and Doreen A. Guenter, "Net and Canadian Libraries: New Telecommunications Facilities for Library and Information Services," *Canadian Journal of Information Science*, June 1982, 1-10.

6. JoAn S. Segal, "Networking and Decentralization." in *Annual Review of Information Science and Technology*, vol. 20, edited by Martha E. Williams. White Plains, N.Y.: Knowledge Industry

Publications, for the American Society for Information Science, 1986, 203-31.

7. Henriette D. Avram, "Network-Level Decisions: Basis and Key Issues," in *Information Technology: Critical Choices for Library Decision-Makers*. Proceedings of a conference, November 1981, Pittsburgh, Pa. New York: Marcel Dekker, 1982.

8. Thomas J. Ballard, *The Failure of Resource Sharing in Public Libraries and Alternative Strategies for Service*. Chicago, Ill.: American Library Association, 1986.

Part 2: *Tradition, Technology, and the Reference Function*

How Can Online Database Searching Be Integrated with Traditional Reference Services?

TINA ROOSE
Director, Systems Reference Service
North Suburban Library System
Wheeling, Illinois

How can online database searching be integrated with traditional reference services? First, what do we mean by integration? In my view, it means creating an environment in which we use remote, dial-up databases in computerized format just as readily and easily as we use in-house, print, or microform resources. I believe in order to integrate online searching with traditional reference services, we need to be as familiar with online databases as we are with print sources such as *Books in Print, Encyclopedia of Associations, World Almanac, World Book Encyclopedia, Statistical Abstract, Education Index,* and *Readers' Guide*.

How can online database searching be integrated with traditional reference services? Obviously, in even asking this question we are presuming online searching *should* be integrated with traditional reference services. I believe online searching should and can be integrated with traditional reference services in many libraries. I will be the first to say, however, that online searching is not appropriate for every library, just as an online circulation system is not appropriate for every library. Remember, the *majority* of public libraries in this country have budgets under $50,000, very few staff, and often only one reference person. (I do believe, however, that some of those smaller libraries *can* get access to online searching through cooperative arrangements with other libraries or library systems.)

Assuming your library is interested in offering your clientele direct on site access to the 700 or so computer databases now readily available, how do you integrate use of these resources with the resources you already have? I could suggest guidelines for such integration of resources. I could suggest an overriding guideline like: *Make online resources as easy to use and as readily available as print resources*. That simplifies and confuses in the same breath.

All of us interpret such general guidelines in many different ways depending on our staffs, budgets, and physical plants. I've seen many enthusiastic and well-meaning librarians (both reference staff and administrators) initiate online searching in their libraries, knowing that these new resources would give their patrons more, faster, and better access to information. I've seen some of those same librarians become frustrated and concerned when they find their library doing only a few online searches a month. "Why?" they ask. "Why are we doing so few searches a month? It's hard to keep up our search skills when we do so few searches. We are afraid the quality of our service will deteriorate and that we are wasting valuable resources." They are right. The quality of their online searching will deteriorate and they will have wasted valuable staff time as well as money on training and equipment. Obviously, in these libraries, online searching is not integrated with their traditional reference services. In these libraries, online searching barely exists. Even if both management and staff want to do online searching, barriers still exist. Even in libraries that do many online searches, online searching is often underused because of such barriers.

What are some of the barriers? Barriers fall into three basic categories: human, monetary, and physical. Ultimately, both the monetary and physical barriers are determined by humans. Therefore, the primary barrier is human. It's us. It's we. Some of these barriers are deliberate. Some of these barriers are unintentional. But, just as with racial integration, the unintentional barriers are equally effective in preventing integration of online resources.

It doesn't matter that there is no official policy that says "Don't do many online searches." If only two of the five reference staff have had online training, how many searches will that library do? If staff are not given time or money to practice searching, how many searches will that library do? If the library charges all search costs to the patrons, how many searches will that library do? If the librarians will only do searches for patrons who specifically request them, how many searches will that library do? If the library will only do searches by appointment, how many searches will that library do? If the administration will not let staff use online sources for ready reference, how many searches will that library do? These are examples of policies, official or unofficial, deliberate or not, which serve as barriers and restrict the use of online resources.

Let's look more closely at one of these barriers--staff training and expertise. Many library managers are unrealistic about how much training and practice staff need to search online databases as expertly and readily as print sources. I think back to my year in library school. How many resources did I learn about during that year? Thirty? Sixty? One hundred? Whatever the number, it was far fewer than the number of computer databases we are trying to learn about in one or two days' worth of training and whatever practice time some of us are allowed. And in that one or two days' worth of training and library-allotted practice time, we have to learn not only new resources but also new languages, foreign languages with which to access those resources--the foreign languages of vendors like BRS or Dialog or Wilson.

How to overcome this barrier? Staff need active encouragement and support from management. Give staff plenty of practice time. Let staff initiate searches. Encourage them to try online databases for many questions just to find out what information is in those databases and how it is arranged. Give them money and time to do so. It doesn't work to say "Search all you want" and in the same breath, "But be very careful about how much it costs." It doesn't work to say "Search all you want" and never give them any free time to do so. Staff are smart. They interpret both the verbal and the nonverbal messages you give about their learning process. Your permission isn't sufficient: they need your active, visible commitment to their learning.

So far I've been focusing on human and monetary barriers to integration of online searching. What about the physical barriers? I think a primary physical barrier is the location of the computer or terminal used for online searching. If the search machine is not easily accessible to reference staff at all times, how can that staff possibly use it as readily or as well as a print source? Having the search computer in another room or on another floor is often an example of an unintentional barrier. Of course, having the search machine in a remote location could also be an example of a deliberate barrier. Whoever makes the decision about where to put the machine may KNOW and HOPE (secretly) that distance breeds contempt. Whoever makes the decision about location may be trying to control costs in an indirect way. But that kind of indirect cost control may just result in sabotaging online searching--and costing the library money for wasted equipment or training.

What if your attitude is that you believe online databases should be treated similarly to print resources? Okay, then don't lock up theses resources in some back room or basement cranny. People in some libraries tell me they can't do online searches in a public area, that they can't concentrate. Yet these same people manage to search *Education Index* or *Readers Guide* in a public area. Why the difference? I believe very strongly that if staff were given enough time and encouragement to practice searching computer databases, they would be able to search them as easily and as fast as print sources.

I'm reiterating because I believe we often underestimate the effects of the attitudes and decisions of library managers. Library managers can unintentionally sabotage many a new service. Library managers must remember that staff can't be expected to search unfamiliar equipment without lots of support and encouragement. When I say support and encouragement, I mean concrete things like allocating both time and money for staff to learn about these new sources.

If all the reference librarians are already overworked (and of course, underpaid) as in many libraries, how can they be expected to take on the responsibility for learning about these new sources without some shift in their old responsibilities?

Some staff may be reluctant to search if they think each search means fewer books added to the collection. Discussion among all staff is necessary.

If the search machine is not near the reference desk, how can the one librarian on duty leave the area to do a computer search? If we want to get maximum use from a source, it must be nearby. How many libraries have a small collection of most used reference sources within arm's reach of the reference desk? If we want truly to integrate the use of online sources with traditional print sources, we need to have our computer search machine within arm's reach also.

Proximity breeds familiarity, and familiarity breeds use. It's a simple law of human nature. We go first and most often to the sources we know best. The more barriers put between us and our resources, the less likely we are to use them. If library managers erect physical, monetary, or human barriers (like not training enough staff or having enough staff on hand) they cannot expect staff to use fully these new computer resources.

Access to computerized resources helps us give more and better and faster service. But to do so demands commitment, both from management and staff. Staff who are committed to excellent service cannot provide it without sufficient backing from the library management.

What about libraries that do many searches already? Many of the things I've already said apply to them as well. Some other libraries, especially very large or very busy libraries, may do many online searches but still not really integrate online searching with the rest of their reference services. Online searching is often viewed as a new separate service, a specialized service for which patrons must pay. In a way, these libraries are upgrading those paying patrons to first class, leaving the rest of the patrons in coach class. Only those paying patrons will get access to the total resources of that library. One reason the smaller libraries may be doing few searches could be that they subscribe to this same classist philosophy that only them that's got, gets.

So a primary reason for underuse of online databases could be the attitude of the administration. If they insist on charging patrons for searches, how many searches will be done in an average library? Of course, in a large university many searches can be paid for from faculty grants. If the university does searches for people in the community, many private businesses can write off the costs. My concern is that the main clientele for searches will be those with money, leaving poorer students and faculty and community members without access.

In large public libraries we can see the same scenario. But what about the average academic, public, school, or special library? The majority of their clientele will request online searches if they have to pay for them. We have seen many examples of this phenomenon both locally and nationally. Many libraries that charge their patrons all search costs did very few searches. In those libraries, the staff lost both their expertise and their courage to try computer databases. And what kind of service did patrons who were willing to pay get if staff skills were rusty? It's obviously a vicious circle. The fewer searches we do the less skill we have and the worse (and less cost effective) service we give. Some of those libraries that charged fees for online searching have now dropped all or part of their fees. The result is they are doing more searches and have more skill.

To recap some important questions to ask when trying to integrate online searching with traditional reference services:

1. Costs of searching: Who pays? If patrons pay search costs, searches will be fewer and only clients with money will have access.

2. Who initiates search? If patrons must ask for search, you'll do less searching. Patrons don't have to ask for you to search the *World Almanac* or *Books in Print* or *Readers' Guide,* do they?

3. How is resource used? Is it used for ready reference or only for in-depth research?

4. Must patrons make an appointment for a search?

5. How comfortable are staff with these online resources?

6. How much training and how much practice time have they been given to learn about these sources?

7. How easy to use are the search machine and your communications software?

8. Location of search machine. How close is it to the reference desk? How convenient is it to use?

What will keep us from successfully integrating online searching with traditional reference services? Philosophy is the key. Our philosophy determines our behavior which determines what barriers to integration we erect. It is common sense that if we want this group of computerized resources to be used, we must minimize the barriers to their use.

I said earlier that some of these barriers may be deliberate, some may be unintentional. The end results are the same. These results include: 1) Online searching is underutilized and not as cost effective as it could be; 2) Staff skill and knowledge are less, resulting in lower quality and quantity reference service; 3) Staff morale is lower, which could also result in both lower quality and lower quantity reference service; 4) Library loses the public relations benefit of doing computer searching; and, most important, 5) Patrons lose the benefits of access to these wonderful resources.

Improving the Accessibility of Library Resources

KAREN MARKEY
Assistant Professor
School of Information and Library Studies
The University of Michigan
Ann Arbor, Michigan

Four developments are now taking shape that could improve the accessibility of library resources for patrons and staff:

- Availability of the machine-readable Library of Congress Subject Headings (LCSH-mr)
- Availability of machine-readable library classifications
- Automatic scanning and conversion of printed text into machine-readable form for enhanced subject description
- Availability of machine-readable reference databases.

The positive and negative aspects of each of these four developments are features in this paper. Economic consideration, although important, will not be considered in detail here. With appropriate resolution of negative aspects, these four developments will substantially benefit library patrons and staff by:

- Increasing the efficiency and accuracy of subject cataloging and classification
- Enhancing subject access in both online cataloging systems and online catalogs.

Machine-readable Library of Congress Subject Headings

Background

The online catalog improvement most often requested by surveyed online catalog users in the CLR-sponsored Online Catalog Project was the "ability to view a list of words related to my search words" (Matthews, Lawrence, and Ferguson 1983). To aid subject searches, online catalog system designers have introduced alphabetical browsing displays of assigned subject headings. A few systems offer keyword searching subject headings. Such keyword searching results in browsing displays of retrieved headings (Lawrence 1985). A few online catalog designs have recently introduced a searching capability which allows users to selected an assigned subject heading in a retrieved record to find additional records bearing the assigned headings (Markey, in press). These approaches exploit subject headings assigned to a syndetic structure or semantic relationships between subject headings found in the printed or microfiche editions of the *Library of Congress Subject Headings*.

The principal reason that *LCSH* has not been considered in online catalog design and functionability has been the lack of an up-to-date LCSH in machine-readable form (LCSH-mr). The library community has encouraged LC to make an up-to-date LCSH-mr available. In 1981, the Subject Analysis Committee (SAC) of the American Library Association (ALA) appointed the ad hoc subcommittee on Library of Congress Subject Authority Control. The subcommittee's principal recommendation was that the "Library of Congress should distribute a machine-readable subject authority file in the MARC authorities Format and provide periodic updates which are easily integrated into the base file" (American Library Association 1982). The top priority action identified at the

Subject Access Meeting which was sponsored by the Council on X Resources and help in Dublin, Ohio, in June 1982 was to "create and distribute in machine-readable form the *Library of Congress Subject Headings (LCSH)* in the LC-MARC authority format providing for *current* and *regular* updates" (Jones 1983, 117).

In April 1986, an up-to-date LCSH-mr was published by the Library of Congress in the form of a cumulative master tape and weekly tape update service ("MARC Distribution Service" 1986). The ongoing publication and update of LCSH-mr will soon be accompanied by the development of subject authority capabilities in bibliographic utilities and integrated library systems.

LCSH-mr for Online Cataloging Systems

The inclusion of LCSH-mr in centralized online cataloging systems will enable subject catalogers to access the most current version of LCSH in the form of subject authority records. Such enhanced systems will also provide catalogers with the ability to search bibliographic records and/or subject authority records in various ways (keyword, alphabetical) when they assign subject headings to library materials. To facilitate comparisons with their own efforts, catalogers will have the subject heading practice of libraries expressed in millions of bibliographic records at their fingertips. In addition, access to the current version of the controlled vocabulary through subject authority files will increase the quality, consistency, and accuracy of subject heading assignment in centralized online cataloging system records.

A fraction of assigned subject headings in a library's bibliographic records will be found among subject authority records in LCSH-mr. Cochrane (1986, 13-19) gives reasons for this: (a) catalogers' addition of free-floating subdivisions to main headings by following rules in the divisions manual (X of Congress 1981), (b) catalogers' assignment of subdivisions and references to a heading governed by a model or pattern heading, (c) out-of-date headings from previous LCSH editions, (d) catalogers' assignment of unauthorized main headings and/or subdivisions, (e) spelling and typographical errors, and (f) subfield coding errors.

Experimentation with computerized error correction algorithms has demonstrated that spelling, typographical, and subfield coding errors can be automatically corrected (O'Neill and Vizine-Goetz 1982). The incorporation of subject authority records for free-floating subdivisions into online cataloging systems could help catalogers in the construction of assigned subject headings. However, LC has no plans to convert free-floating subdivisons into machine-readable form and distribute authority records for these subdivisions.

Now that LCSH-mr is available, a significant development effort is needed by bibliographic utilities to incorporate LCSH-mr into their systems, link these records with their related bibliographic records, and offer capabilities for subject searching, browsing, and display of both authority records and related bibliographic records. It will not be sufficient for utilities to treat subject authority records like bibliographic records and add the former into searchable indexes and databases without making links between related bibliographic records and other subject authority records.

Links between subject authority records will enable catalogers to explore the syndetic structure of LCSH. When catalogers find a candidate subject heading, they can follow the links from the heading's subject authority record to bibliographic records, and examine retrieved bibliographic records to determine whether the candidate heading is appropriate to assign to the bibliographic record for the book at hand. Conversely, catalogers can first search bibliographic records to find an appropriate subject heading to assign to the book in hand, retrieve the subject authority record for the candidate heading and examine its cross reference structure to determine if a better heading is available to represent the books' subject contents.

The Subject Cataloging Division issues changed, deleted, and new subject authority records on a weekly basis through a tape subscription service. Bibliographic utilities will have to maintain and update subject authority records in the centralized system. Utilities could also be libraries' source for obtaining changed, deleted, or new subject authority records to add to their local systems. This will enable libraries to keep the cross reference structure in their online catalogs current and consistent with that of the Library of Congress.

LCSH-mr in Online Catalogs

Integrated library system vendors and library systems staff now have the opportunity to respond to online catalog users' need for related terms by incorporating LCSH-mr into their local systems. There will be few instances, however, when related terms from LCSH-mr are displayed in their online catalog searches. Two reasons for this are: (a) few patron searches enter subject access points that match subject headings or "see" references in LCSH (Markey 1984, 66; Markey and Demeyer 1986, 232-36), and (b) few searchers know that the subjects represented in the library catalog are generated from a controlled vocabulary (Pritchard 1981; Steinberg and Metz 1984).

Systems staff need to design and implement links between assigned subject headings and LCSH-mr; such links are necessary to associate the assigned headings with LCSH-mr subject authority records bearing related terms. They also must design and implement automatic techniques (such as spelling correction algorithms, search trees, and implicit truncation) that will transform patron-entered terms into search terms that match assigned subject headings or headings in LCSH-mr. Once a match has been made, systems can respond with related term lists from subject authority records and/or bibliographic records bearing the matched heading.

The task of maintaining and updating local subject authority records when LC changes, adds, or deletes headings will be eased by a global change capability in the authority control functions of integrated library systems. Yet, few bibliographic utilities have mounted LCSH-mr in their systems or provided libraries with the capability for maintaining and updating local subject authority records when changes occur. UTLAS provides such a capability for libraries' whose bibliographic records are in their database. Until an updating service exists, libraries will have at least two options: (1) replying on the *Weekly Lists* to manually edit local subject authority records, or (2) periodically rebuilding their local subject authority file by processing their bibliographic database against

LCSH-mr themselves or through a vendor's authority control service.

When designing displays for cross references in subject authority records that will be accessed by patron searches, library systems staff and integrated library system vendors may choose to represent the w-subfield coding in "see also form" reference fields with labels for "related," "narrower," and "broader" subject headings. LC instructs that "no intellectual evaluation of the references was introduced in 1985, these designations in many cases will be incorrect" ("Cross Reference Structure" 1986, 62). Thus, the designations "narrower," "broader," and "related" will not express relationships that have been established editorially, and labels generated from w-subfield coding will be, consequently, suspect.

Summary

The availability of LCSH-mr provides us with the opportunity to improve online bibliographic systems with what users want most--the ability to view a list of words related to their search words. The incorporation of LCSH-mr in online cataloging systems should enable library staff to perform subject cataloging tasks online. These systems should also convey changes in LCSH-mr to library staff. Then staff can keep the cross reference structure of their local systems current with that of the Library of Congress. To build LCSH-mr into an effective online tool, system designers must incorporate subject searching and browsing capabilities and user assistance features that reveal the relationships among subject headings.

Machine-readable Library Classifications

Background

Not all aspects of the cataloging process have been aided by the computer-based systems that were introduced in the middle 1960s. While recent developments have accelerated efforts to build and improve files for different formats of machine-readable cataloging records and the related files of authority records, there has been, unfortunately, little parallel effort to automate the file of classification schedules, tables, and indexes that controls the shelf arrangement of library materials. This arrangement, that is, shelflist order, is a more systematic and logical arrangement of records than an alphabetical list of subject headings. If properly exhibited online, this arrangement may become useful for browsing displays for the information seeker (Cochrane and Markey 1985) and an added source of subject information for indexing in online bibliographic systems and access by the information seeker.

The findings of the CLR-sponsored Online Catalog Project conducted in 1982 showed that library patrons wanted subject searching improvements made to the online catalog. In response to the CLR findings, researchers at the OCLC Online Computer Library Center in Dublin, Ohio, studied the Decimal Classification (DDC) incorporating it in an online catalog as a patron searching tool for subject access, browsing, and display (Markey and Demeyer 1986). The DDC Online Project was supported by the Council on Library Resources (CLR), OCLC, and Forest Press and used a machine-readable DDC that was converted from computer tapes used originally to produce the nineteenth edition. The machine-readable Schedules and Relative Index were incorporated into the searchable indexes and browsing capabilities of an experimental online catalog. The effectiveness of this online catalog was tested in online retrieval experiments at four participating libraries.

The DDC Online Project demonstrated that the DDC enhanced both subject access and the display of subject-rich information in bibliographic records. The DDC described the subject matter of bookshelf areas where retrieved items in online searches were located. The DDC also provided new and fruitful subject searching and browsing capabilities that are not possible through the alphabetical and keyword searching permitted by existing online catalogs.

A machine-readable format for the DDC was defined by Forest Press and the editorial staff of the Decimal Classification Division (DCD) of LC that can serve as the foundation for a MARC format for library classifications. In figure 1, a machine-readable record is shown for DDC Schedule number 658.3145.

This record and others were incorporated in the experimental online catalog developed in 1984 for the DDC Online Project.

Figure 1. Authority Record for DDc Schedule Number 658.3145

me	658.3145
met	Interpersonal relations
nine	Including informal, day-to-day relations between supervisors and subordinates
not	Promotion of effective working relationships between individuals and groups
Ind	$a Interpersonal relations $b employees $c personnel administration $e general management

The DCD has since made minor changes to the machine-readable format for DDC Schedule and Table records. For example, Relative Index entries bearing the same class number as a Schedule or Table record are now included in these records. DCD is now using these machine-readable records in an online editorial support system to produce the 20th edition of the DDC.

In an independent effort, Williamson (1986) is tackling the problems of representing and converting the Library of Congress Classification (LCC) to machine-readable form.

Library Classifications for Online Cataloging Systems

The 19th edition of the DDC has been converted to machine-readable records to facilitate the editorial and production processes of publishing the 20th edition. Research is now being undertaken to convert LCC to machine-readable form. At the present time, no MARC format for classification authorities exists. Thus, efforts to convert classifications to machine-readable formats should, at least, be coordinated with each other to ensure that the resulting formats are consistent and compatible with each other. Development and research efforts with DDC and LCC indicate that these classifications may be available in machine-readable form from their respective publishers in the near future; however, a MARC format for classification authorities may be needed but not yet established by that time.

The incorporation of machine-readable library classifications into centralized online cataloging systems will enable catalogers to access the most current version of the classification online. Such enhanced systems will also provide catalogers with the ability to search bibliographic records and/or classification authority records in various ways (keyword, alphabetical, class number) when they assign class numbers and subject headings into library materials. Catalogers will have the classification practice of libraries expressed in millions of bibliographic records at their fingertips. Access to the most current version of the classification online combined with the ability to compare one's efforts with other libraries' classification practice can lead to greater standardization and thereby increase the quality, consistency, and accuracy of class number assignment in centralized online cataloging system records, while also discouraging local (nonstandard) practices. For example, local practices in the assignment of classification numbers, especially truncation of class numbers, may be discouraged by access to classification online.

Initially, searching the individual computers of synthesized class numbers will not be possible because such components are not explicitly coded in the classification number fields of bibliographic records. One or more developments are needed to index components of synthesized class numbers: (1) subfield coding of class number components manually entered into the system by library classifiers (Wajenberg 1983), and/or (2) computer parsing of class number components.

To be properly displayed and accessible online, classification schedules need to be systematically and logically arranged and linked to bibliographic records. A significant development effort is needed by bibliographic utilities to incorporate classification number authority records into their systems, link these records with their related bibliographic records, and offer capabilities for subject searching, browsing, and displaying both authority records and related bibliographic records. It will be sufficient for utilities to treat classification number authority records like bibliographic records and add the former into searchable indexes and databases without making links between class numbers in bibliographic records and classification number records.

Links between these records will enable subject catalogers to search classification number records for the topic of a book in hand, retrieve classification records, and display bibliographic records bearing the class number of the former records. Catalogers can then verify that the book in hand will be classed with other library material on the same topic. Conversely, links between these records will enable subject catalogers to search classification number records for the topic of a book in hand, retrieve classification records, and display bibliographic records bearing the class number of the former records. Catalogers can then verify that the book in hand will be classed with other library material on the same topic. Conversely, links between these records will enable subject catalogers to search bibliographic, evaluate the class numbers in these records, and select and appropriate class number to assign to the book in hand.

Utilities must consider means of maintaining and updating library classifications in the centralized system when format changes are introduced, or when new editions, phoenix schedules, and class number changes are introduced to the classification. At the present time, MARC format changes by LC and ALA committees put development teams into action at bibliographic utilities to develop, test, and implement software to make necessary changes to the online system. Utilities announce system and format changes to their members in written technical bulletins and install system changes. This approach could serve as a model for utilities' maintenance and update of format changes to library classifications. However, new editions, phoenix schedules, and class number changes may require changes to class numbers in bibliographic records. Utilities will probably not change class numbers of the bibliographic records in their cataloging databases, but they will need to convey this information to libraries who have incorporated a library classification into their local system and who choose to reclassify their collections with the most current version of the classification.

Library Classifications for Online Catalogs

The DDC Online Project demonstrated that the incorporation of library classifications in online catalogs offers library patrons and staff enhanced subject access to bibliographic records, enhanced displays of subject-rich catalog information, and improved browsing capabilities. Existing online catalogs can be enhanced with searching, browsing, and display capabilities comparable to those employed in and recommended by the DDC Online Project to handle the library classification enlisted by the library.

A significant development effort is need by integrated library system vendors or library systems staff to incorporate classification number authority records into online catalogs, link these records with their related bibliographic records, and offer capabilities for subject searching, browsing, and display of both authority and bibliographic records. Development staff must also take into account maintenance and update of the former records and related bibliographic records to ensure that their local system contains the most up-to-date version of the classification. Library staff will have to decide whether to reclassify library material when new editions, phoenix schedules, and class number changes are published. Global change capabilities in the local system will facilitate changes to class numbers in bibliographic records. However, staff will still have to fetch library materials, update their call number labels, and reshelve the materials. Some libraries may opt to change the class number that is indexed in their local system, but not change the call number label on the actual material. This practice will not maintain the systematic order of materials on library shelves. It will, however, maintain the systematic order of bibliographic records in the local catalog and reduce staff time required by changing call number labels on material.

Libraries that have established local practices that deviate from the current edition(s) of a library classification may not find that incorporating a library classification in their local system will improve subject access to the catalog. In fact, libraries that have consistently truncated class numbers and placed items in general class numbers may find that incorporating a classification in their online catalog will adversely affect retrieval. For example, when catalogers lump all "football" books in 796.332 instead of specific numbers, patrons' searches for specific topics such as "Superbowl," "Football at Florida State University," or "defense in football" will result in a large number of retrievals of all books that bear the DDC class number 796.332. Libraries using a previous edition of the classification or a local revision of the classification may find that incorporating a library classification in their local system will adequately represent the classification practice in their library.

Summary

Online access to machine-readable library classifications is not as far along as online access to LCSH-mr, but there are signs that machine-readable library classifications will be available in the near future. An editorial support system has been installed in the Decimal Classification Division to enable the DDC editors to produce the 20th edition of DDC using machine-readable classification records of the 19th edition. Forest Press supported a research project in which these records were incorporated into an online catalog and searched by library patrons and staff in retrieval experiments. Research is now being undertaken to represent and convert LCC to machine-readable form. A MARC format for classification authorities has yet to be defined and established.

The incorporation of machine-readable library classifications in centralized online cataloging systems will enable staff to perform classification tasks online. The centralized system should also convey changes to the classification to library staff. Then libraries can keep the classification in their local systems current; however, additional staff time may be required to change call number labels on the actual books. To build the library classification into an effective online tool, system designers must incorporate subject searching and browsing capabilities and user assistance features that take advantage of the logical structure of the classification.

Conversion of Printed Text into Machine-Readable Form

Background

In the CLR-sponsored Online Catalog Project, users were asked to select additional online catalog features from a list of fourteen choices. The second-ranked feature was the ability to search a book's table of contents, summary, or index (Matthews, Lawrence, and Ferguson 1983). Since 1978, a number of separate research projects have shown that bibliographic records enhanced with subject-rich terms from books' tables of contents and/or indexes improve users' ability to retrieve subject information.

The findings of the Subject Access Project (SAP) at Syracuse University (Atherton 1978) demonstrated that enhancement of bibliographic records with terms from books' tables of contents and indexes produced a useful vocabulary for online subject searching. Enhanced bibliographic records were entered in an experimental database of MARC-like records called BOOKS. When SAP researchers compared online searches of BOOKS with searches performed against MARC records alone, they concluded that BOOKS searches took less time, retrieved more relevant items, and were more precise. Furthermore, users found some items in BOOKS which would have been impossible to locate through LC subject headings or through subject-rich terms in title fields.

At Lund University in Sweden, Wormell (1981) applied SAP indexing techniques to a database of records for four hundred books in the field of environmental protection and ecology. In a retrieval experiment similar to the one performed with the BOOKS database, Wormell demonstrated that the test database permitted detailed subject access and was cost-effective because the indexing terminology was taken from the books themselves. In a follow-up experiment, Wormell (1985) applied SAP indexing method to create a database of Swedish Government Official Reports (Statens Offentlig Utredningar or SOU); the database is currently maintained by the Swedish government.

Extending the research on enhanced subject descriptions, Markey and Calhoun (in press) analyzed the subject-rich fields in bibliographic records to determine the average number of unique words (excluding stopwords) contributed successively by these fields.

When bibliographic records from four libraries' databases were screened to include only records bearing bibliographic contents and/or summary notes (MARC fields 505 and 520), between 3 and 5 percent of the records in the libraries' databases were included in the analysis. Subject headings contributed an average of 4.84 unique words, while the contents and summary notes fields contributed an average of 15.50 unique words per record. The researchers concluded that libraries should consider integrating contents and summary notes into their online catalogs, since these are major contributors of subject-rich words.

Enhanced bibliographic databases are now being developed and maintained by for-profit firms for online searching by commercial retrieval system users and by libraries for searching by online catalog users. In the United States, a commercial database named "Superindex" is available in which an indexing approach similar to SAP has been employed to enhance access to selected reference books, in the fields of science, engineering, and medicine (Starkoff 1984). At the Purdue University Engineering Library, library staff copy tables of contents and book indexes, a professional librarian scans each and marks appropriate headings, and student assistants input these headings into a local online catalog (Posey and Erdmann 1986). The staff at the Australia Defence Force Academy photocopy tables of contents and books' indexes, select either the contents or index, select appropriate words or phrases, and input these into a local online catalog (Byrne 1986).

Automatic Conversion of Printed Text for Enhanced Subject Description

Previously, the development of bibliographic databases containing enhanced bibliographic records has required manual input of the enhancements. In other words, project or library staff have manually keyed subject-rich terms from tables of contents, indexes, and other summary information drawn from books into automated systems. SAP researchers at both Syracuse and Lund Universities concluded that the costs of creating enhanced records were not prohibitive. Automatic conversion of printed text into machine-readable form, however, can reduce the man-hours needed to manually input subject-rich terms books' tables of contents or indexes into automated systems.

An intelligent optical scanning technique has been developed by a British company, OPTIRAM, to scan written or printed text and convert it to machine-readable form. OPTIRAM has an exceptionally high accuracy rate of 99.98 percent which is attributed to its analysis of words rather than individual characters. Harrison (1985) describes automatic retrospective conversion of a library's card catalog using OPTIRAM as the scanning component of the operation and LIBPAC as the MARC format recognition component of this retrospective conversion operation is indicative of the potential of this technology to automatically convert books' tables of contents and indexes to machine-readable form.

In a report on current online catalog developments and enhancements, Hildreth (in press) describes how OPTIRAM is now being employed in a British Library-sponsored project to scan books' title pages and tables of contents and convert these texts to machine-readable form. Software will be developed and implemented to compare scanned title page data with the contents of MARC fields containing title page information (for example, MARC-tagged fields 245, 250, 260) in BLAISE-LINE records (The British Library's online cataloging system) and to identify the one bibliographic record bearing the scanned data. Then, the machine-readable tables of contents will be added to this record and indexed in the system. Enlisting OPTIRAM and related software for automatic BLAISE-LINE searching and enhancement of bibliographic records may significantly reduce the costs involved in enhancing records, because the labor-intensive manual keying of additional subject data is not needed.

When bibliographic records are enhanced with subject information, libraries must increase the amount of computer storage in their local systems. Also, the subject searching capabilities and user assistance features of existing online catalogs may not be sufficient for handling patron searches in an enhanced database.

For example, a patron interested in finding a book on the Italian Renaissance performs a subject search for "Italian Renaissance." In an enhanced bibliographic database, such a search would result in records for books and book chapters on this topic.

The online catalog must be equipped with assistance to direct the patron to the most suitable item(s).

Summary

Online catalog users have expressed their desire to search books' tables of contents, summaries, or indexes in the online catalog. Research project have demonstrated that bibliographic records enhanced with subject-rich terms from books improve searchers' ability to retrieve subject information. At least four organizations are now regularly enhancing bibliographic records and making this information searchable in commercial databases or online catalogs. The development of these enhanced bibliographic databases, however, has required manual input of enhancements. An intelligent optical scanning and conversion technique like OPTIRAM offers an alternative to manual input of enhancements. Written or printed text can now be automatically scanned and converted to machine-readable form. This may significantly reduce the costs involved in enhancing records and open the door to additional efforts by commercial firms, vendors, bibliographic utilities, national cataloging agencies, and/or libraries to enhance bibliographic records with the subject information in library materials.

Reference Databases in the Online Catalog

The online catalog has more potential than simply serving as the source of bibliographic information about a library's collection. In the CLR-sponsored Online Catalog Project, catalog users participating in focused group interviews wanted to search the online catalog for the titles of individual articles in journals, and for the text of newspapers articles. They also wanted to be able to search certain periodical indexes and reference works such as *Reader's Guide to Periodical Literature, Magazine Index*, and *Keesing's Archives*, in the online catalog (Markey 1984).

Over six dozen encyclopedias, reference books, law codes, and newspaper and periodical indexes are now available for purchase or demonstration on CD-ROM discs ("CD-ROM disc Titles" 1986).

The availability of these discs indicates publisher's willingness to distribute machine-readable text, indexes, directories, and databases. Evaluation of CD-ROM discs and workstations have noted libraries' reluctance to invest in this new technology because different hardware and software are usually necessary to handle individual discs (Van Arsdale and Ostrye 1986). With this limitation in mind, libraries may opt to incorporate these data in their local systems in the same database as their bibliographic records or in separate databases.

If these reference data are incorporated, existing online catalogs will need additional user assistance features for guiding patrons from their inquiry to the best or a suitable source of information. Patrons will also need special assistance to operate in an online environment with multiple thesauri or controlled vocabularies. Reference databases will almost certainly include entries for articles in periodicals and newspapers to which the library does not subscribe. The library will thus need to determine whether to load the entire database into their online catalog and provide user assistance for locating materials they do not own, or to load only those entries referring to periodicals and newspapers to which they subscribe.

Similarly, in the case of encyclopedias and reference books, should only those bibliographic references for materials that are in the library's collection be added to the online catalog? Incorporating reference databases in libraries' local systems will require the resolution of these and other difficult and challenging issues, but the availability of these databases represents the opportunity to transform the library catalog into a gateway to library resources.

Conclusion

The four developments described in this paper offer libraries great potential for improving accessibility to their resources. However, significant design and development efforts by bibliographic utilities, library systems staff, and integrated system vendors are required to handle:

- LCSH-mr

- Machine-readable library classification

- Automatic enhancement of MARC records and searching of these enhanced records

- Selection and inclusion of entries form machine-readable reference databases.

Each entails different subject searching and browsing capabilities and user assistance features. Incorporating a machine-readable library classification, LCSH-mr, enhanced MARC records, and reference databases will require increased computer storage. Libraries will have to consider the issues of retrospective conversion, recataloging, reclassification, and even relabeling of library materials to ensure that the classification numbers and subject headings in bibliographic records agree with the latest edition of the classification of LCSH. If libraries start enhancing bibliographic records of recently acquired material, what will they do with previously cataloged material? How can the online catalog convey to patron users the coverage and scope of reference databases in view of what the library holds on site?

This paper has described both negative and positive aspects of incorporating additional bibliographic data and subject-rich information in the online catalog. Often, the negative aspects seem to outweigh the positive ones. Yet, computer technology now provides us with the opportunity and technical capability to reach beyond catalog objectives about subject access to books formulated over one hundred years ago. We can now respond to needs expressed by library patrons and staff regarding subject access and browsing, and the scope and coverage of the library catalog. The library catalog can now be transformed from a finding device into a gateway to library collections and accommodate the rising expectations of catalog users

References

American Library Association. Subject Analysis Committee. Ad hoc Subcommittee on Library of Congress Subject Authority Control. 1982. "Library of Congress Subject Authority Control: Scope, Format and Distribution."

Atherton, Pauline. 1978. *Books Are for Use: Final Report of the Subject Access Project to the Council on Library Resources.* Syracuse, N.Y.: Syracuse University.

Byrne, Alex. 1986. "Life Wasn't Meant to Be Whimsical: Painless Subject Augmentation." *Australasian College Libraries* 42:83-90.

"CD-ROM Disc Titles." 1986. *CD-ROM Review*, no. 1.

Cochrane, Pauline. 1986. *Improving LCSH in Online Catalogs.* Littleton, Colo.: Libraries Unlimited.

Cochrane, Pauline A., and Karen Markey. 1985. "Preparing for the Use of Classification in Online Cataloging Systems and in Online Catalogs." *Information Technology and Libraries* 4, no. 2:91-111.

"Cross Reference Structure and the LC Automated Subject Authority File." *Cataloging Service Bulletin* 33:62.

Harrison, Martin. 1985. "Retrospective Conversion of Card Catalogues into Full MARC Format Using Sophisticated Computer-Controlled Visual Imaging Techniques." *Program* 19, no. 3:213-30.

Hildreth, Charles R. "Beyond Boolean: Designing the Next Generation of Online Catalogs." *Library Trends*. In press.

Jones, C. Lee. 1983. "Summary Recommendations from Subject Access Meeting." *Information Technology and Libraries* 2, no. 1:16-33.

Library of Congress. 1981. *Library of Congress Subject Headings: A Guide to Subdivision Practice*. Washington, D.C.: Library of Congress, Subject Cataloging Division.

MARC Distribution Service--Subject Authorities. 1986. Washington, D.C.: Library of Congress. Press release (March).

Markey, Karen. 1984. *Subject Searching in Library Catalogs: Before and After the Introduction of Online Catalogs.* Dublin, Ohio: OCLC.

Markey, Karen. "Keyword Searching in an Online Catalog Enhanced with a Library Classification." In *Processings of the RTSD- and LITA-sponsored Preconference on Classification, Chicago, 1985 July 4-5.* In press.

Markey, Karen, and Karen Calhoun. *Unique Words Contributed by MARC Records with Summary and/or Contents Notes*. In press.

Markey, Karen, and Anh Demeyer. 1986. *Dewey Decimal Classification Online Project: Evaluation of a Library Classification Schedule and Index Integrated Into the Subject Searching Capabilities of an Online Catalog.* OCLC Research Report Services, no. OCLC/OPR/RR--86/1. Dublin, Ohio: OCLC.

Matthews, Joseph R., Gary S. Lawrence, and Douglas Ferguson. 1983. *Using Online Catalogs: A Nationwide Study*. New York: Neal-Schuman.

O'Neill, Edward T., and Diane Vizine-Goetz. 1982. "Computer Generation of an Authority File." In *Information Interaction*. Proceedings of the 45th ASIS Annual Meeting, 1982 October 17-21, Columbus, Ohio, ed. Anthony E. Petrarca, Celianna I. Taylor, and Robert S. Kohn, 220-23. White Plains, N.Y.: Knowledge Industry Publication.

Posey, Edwin D., and Charlotte A. Erdmann. 1986. "An Online UNIX-based Engineering Library Catalog: Purdue University Engineering Library." *Science and Technology Libraries* 6, no. 4:31-43.

Pritchard, Sarm M. 1981. *SCORPIO: A Study of Public Users of the Library of Congress Information System*. Washington, D.C.: Library of congress.

Starkoff, B. J. 1984. "Superindex: Today and Tomorrow." Paper presented at annual meeting of the Society for Scholarly Publishing, 31 May 1984.

Steinberg, David, and Paul Metz. 1984. "User Response to and Knowledge about an Online Catalog." *College & Research Libraries* 45, no. 1:61-70.

Van Arsdale, William O., and Anne T. Ostrye. 1986. "Infotrac: A Second Opinion." *American Libraries* 17, no. 7: 514-15.

Wajenberg, Arnold. 1983. "MARC Coding of DDC for Subject Retrieval." *Information Technology and Libraries* 2, no. 3:246-51.

Williamson, Nancy J. 1986. "Library of Congress Classification: Problems and Prospects in Online Retrieval." *International Cataloging* 15, no. 4:45-48.

Wormell, Irene. 1981. "SDAP--A New Way to Produce Subject Descriptions of Books." *Journal of Information Science* 3:39-43.

Wormell, Irene. 1985. "SOU-database: Retrieval of Factual Data." In *Subject Access Project--SAP--Improved Subject Retrieval for Monographic Publications*. Ph.D. diss., Lund University.

The Online Catalog: Reference/User Friend or Foe?

DALE K. CARRISON
Director
Minnesota State University System
Project for Automated Library Systems
Mankato State University
Mankato, Minnesota

The theme of this conference, "Changing Technology: Opportunity and Challenge," is especially pertinent at this time in the evolution of online library automation systems. Not only are the business aspects of library automation in a volatile state (with all the mergers, bankruptcies, and other organizational changes now occurring among commercial vendors of automated systems), but the technology and level of expectation of automated library systems is also rapidly changing. The sophistication and ease of use of the average online catalog today is considerably different than it was just eight years ago when MSUS/PALS was started in Minnesota. Jaye Bausser (1981) stated:

> What was once an almost utopian ideal has become an acknowledged necessity for some. The desire to provide faster and more flexible access to the library's collection, the enticement of Boolean searching, the ease of changing and updating

> access points, the integration with other library functions such as acquisitions and circulation, and the capability of linking with other libraries for resource sharing make the online catalog especially attractive for libraries that manage large, complex, bibliographic files and for all libraries that want to provide the utmost in bibliographic access and service.

He was a bit ahead of most of his colleagues in 1981, but not in the contemporary library world of today. Applications of technology to information retrieval are indeed an essential component of any library's services if that library wishes to provide high level information access and retrieval services. My personal view of library automation is that it is a necessity for libraries of all types, that it plays a pervasive role in the total library operation, that a totally integrated system is essential, and that automation is "the only way to go" in terms of the role that libraries should have in society today.

At this point, perhaps I should briefly describe the context in which I work in order that you understand the basis for my thoughts and observations related to library automation. MSUS/PALS is a cooperative network of 28 libraries and 2 sites without libraries, which are a university without a campus (uses community facilities) and MINITEX (the Minnesota Interlibrary Telecommunications Exchange, which is a library network serving all libraries in Minnesota, North Dakota, and South Dakota). The 28 libraries include 6 state universities, 18 community colleges, 2 private colleges, the Legislative Reference Library of the State of Minnesota Legislature, and North Dakota State University, all of which are tied via leased phone lines to the central computer site located at Mankato State University. The services currently provided by MSUS/PALS, some of which are cooperative with Unisys Corporation as part of the marketing agreement which MSUS/PALS has with Unisys Corporation for the sale of the PALS online library system software, are shown in figure 1.

Figure 1: Operational Components

Online catalog system

Online circulation system

Online interlibrary loan system

Electronic mail and real-time messaging

Management statistics module (for all existing online systems)

Help module (for all existing online systems)

Report writer for bibliographic and circulation databases

Report writer for record editing functions

Online and offline printing module

Global editing programs

Transaction coding process for PALS MARC record editing through OCLC

Global authority management

Extensive documentation

Instruction and training activities

MARC up-down programs, for I & R, newspaper indexing, legal research correspondence indexing and tax record indexing applications

Unisys PALS Users Group

PC/PALS (numerous applications including library collections, indexing, social services information, conference registration, and document inventory; has catalog, circulation, acquisition, and serials components)

Other components, shown in figure 2, are in testing and/or under development and will become part of the program of MSUS/PALS during the next year.

Figure 2: Development Activities

Acquisitions and serials system (PALS)

Media reservation system (PALS/Unisys)

Name and subject authority management system (PALS/Unisys)

Sperrylink indexing system (Unisys)

OCLC terminal/PALS systgem interface (PALS/Unisys)

International MARC format adaptation (Unisys)

Multiple language capability (Unisys)

Use of hard disk units and LAN (PALS)

Indexing enhancements (PALS)

User training curriculum and courses (Unisys)

PALS control module (Unisys)

Inventory component for circulation system (PALS)

X.25/X.29 protocol applications (PALS)

Online editing/entry module (PALS/Unisys)

CD-ROM applications (PALS/Unisys)

Transaction analysis (PALS)

Collection development analysis (PALS)

AI/expert systems applications (PALS/Unisys)

Gateway telecommunications applications (PALS)

Telefacsimile applications (PALS)

Some pertinent statistics that will give you an overview of the dimensions of the MSUS/PALS operation include:

1. A database of 2.3 million records of which approximately 1.1 million are unique titles.

2. 286 dedicated terminals, plus dial access capability from any telephone at any location, resulting in 85-95,000 transactions per day and more than 1,500 persons using dial access each day.

3. On a typical day more than 18,000 persons use the PALS system, receiving an average transaction response time of less than 2 seconds.

4. 13,760597 transactions were processed in calendar year 1986, of which 1,752,741 were keyword; 391,252 were known author; 485,536 were known title; 205,065 were author/title combination; and 362,482 were known Library of Congress or other authorized subject heading.

Periodic research studies indicate a highly positive user satisfaction with the PALS system by all types of people in all types of libraries. Users find the system easy to learn and easy to use. Because the command structure is simplified and mnemonic, users retain their knowledge of system operation from one time of use to another time, even if the user seldom has occasion to come to the library. Library staff at all levels are enthusiastic about the PALS online library system and are constantly making suggestions for enhancement and expansion of system capabilities. I do not have time during this talk to discuss the PALS system in detail; however, I would welcome the opportunity to expand on these few comments either in response to questions later in the session or as we have the opportunity to talk during the remainder of the conference.

Research into student searching of computer databases indicates that students who know how to do manual searching receive satisfactory results for modest investments in time. In general, students are a bit slower than librarians, use fewer synonyms, and need some assistance with search strategies. If the research process is analyzed, it has a mechanical component, which can be greatly enhanced by computers and printers, and a critical, evaluative component involving formulation of search strategies and analyzing and evaluating sources. An online library system is successful if it is able to translate this research process into a system that provides a powerful, flexible, informative way for users to drive and control the system to their various ends. Online systems should not presume what these ends are or channel the user according to predefined and required routes. Library users know best what they do and need, although sometimes they also need considerable professional help. Library systems designers know best what the system can do. The goal is to achieve an optimum mix of these two points of view. This process requires constant trade-offs and modification, but it can result in a highly effective and efficient information access and retrieval system.

Ward Shaw (1986) has described the challenge of electronic technology in libraries as the design of a system that enables users to manipulate Aristotelean structures in Platonic forms, that is, driving the systems to explore what users conceive, rather than what system designers have "analyzed in." Libraries have applied Aristotle's methodology with considerable skill and great detail in the construction of classification schemes and MARC records, as well as other elements of cataloging and library design. They have not done so well with the Plato approach of drawing logical conclusions from concepts, however, particularly in the area of information access. Our tools of access have been complex in direct relation to the finiteness of analysis they represent, and require of their users detailed knowledge of both system and discipline structures. Divergence of these two structures is inevitable and very difficult to control. The problem centers on the fact that libraries have forced users to think in the analytic patterns upon which the system is constructed, thus making it very difficult to be creative in their use of the system.

One possible solution to assist users in this process is the use of artificial intelligence. AI is concerned with designing systems that exhibit the characteristics we associate with intelligence in human behavior, including understanding language, learning, reasoning, and solving problems. Areas of application encompassed by artificial intelligence include natural language processing, learning, knowledge representation, automatic programming, expert systems, problem solving, computer vision, speech recognition, and robotics. Several of these areas are relevant to library and information work. For example, natural language processing is useful for end-user searching of online databases. Speech recognition may enable library users to interact with library systems by giving verbal commands instead of entering commands by keyboard. Expert systems, which attempt to codify an expert's knowledge in the form of "if . . . then" rule, are quite likely to be of considerable help to both users and librarians in areas such as cataloging, reference, and library administration.

The use of artificial intelligence concepts in online catalog design is just beginning to be considered by system designers. The field of artificial intelligence is relatively new, with most significant developments taking place in the last two years. Thus, AI is now in the process of becoming a vehicle for the development of a new form of "knowledge media." Knowledge media, according to Mark Stefik, (1986) embrace not only the representation and storage of knowledge, but also its transmission through society. At this point, at least, AI systems are not a major medium for the transmission of knowledge. As AI technology matures, Stefik argues that it will increasingly take on the role of both carrier and transmitter.

AI systems differ from most other knowledge media such as books, diagrams, and films in that they are not entirely frozen and inert. The knowledge in an AI system is dynamic and can be executed for solving problems in a more flexible way than is possible with any other knowledge medium. In this respect, it resembles humans. But so far, the ways in which AI systems can use knowledge to solve problems is still extremely limited as compared with humans. Thus, at this point in time, computer knowledge appears to be far more useful than is computer intelligence for applications in information access and retrieval.

With "know how" programming, experts can convey what they know to be the best way to do something, even though they may never have written it down before. This approach, which utilizes an expert system shell or framework that computerizes an expert's informal rules of thumb as well as formal knowledge, makes it possible for an expert to create a program with minimal help from either programmers or knowledge engineers. Experts can literally train a computer in their field of expertise much as they would an apprentice. Rules of thumb are entered as they occur to the expert, and the program does trial runs to discover logical errors and missing rules by practice. The application of this approach to information access and retrieval provides some exciting and creative design possibilities for the next generation of online catalogs.

It may be useful at this point to look at the basic design of online catalogs in relation to information access and retrieval. Online catalogs do not happen by themselves. Data coming into and going out of the online catalog are processed in various ways, and at each processing point events occur that can influence the nature and effectiveness of searching. Gary Lawrence (1985) identified four design decisions related to the online catalog. First, bibliographic records are processed and stored in the system's database. During this activity most systems create and build indexes continuing the descriptive data extracted from the records. Someone has to decide which parts of each bibliographic record contain data to extract. Thus, the first design decision is "what to search."

Just as bibliographic records are processed by the computer, so is the information entered by the user. Typically, the string of letters typed by the user is "normalized," that is, put into a standard form that the system understands. For example, the user's entry might be converted to upper case, and extra blanks and punctuation removed. The results of this processing are used by the system to conduct the actual search, which means that processing of user input can have an important, and often hidden, effect on searching. Thus, the second design decision involves how to handle the user's input, that is, "what to search with."

The system then executes processes to match the user's input to the contents of the database. It is in this area that most attention to the system design aspects of searching is concentrated. Techniques like keyword searching and the use of Boolean operators would be included here. The third design decision concerns "how to search." The last part of the process is the system's display of the results of the search to the user. This activity reflects decisions about what information to display and in what format. It may be that the manner in which search results are displayed is as influential to success as the methods by which the results are obtained. Thus, the fourth design decision is "how to display search results."

Lawrence suggest four important conclusions based on this context of online catalog design. First, numerous techniques are currently available for use in developing all four areas of design. Second, each of these techniques, examined by itself, has both strengths and weakness. There are no self-evident "right ways" to searching the online catalog. Third, assembling a search method presents risks, because the various techniques interact with and influence each other and do so in many different combinations. Fourth, despite the problems, methods do exist to make effective online catalogs for information access and retrieval, catalogs which are responsive, dynamic, and helpful to all users.

Online catalogs add new dimensions to the traditional problems of access to bibliographic records. The online catalog user encounters command entry difficulties presented by unfriendly interfaces and a bewildering variety of display formats. Different indexing policies for the same machine-readable bibliographical record also govern access. Unfortunately, there are no policies and standards for indexing. Usually, locally adopted or assumed indexing policies determine how indexing is implemented. Index control should be of equal importance to bibliographic control. Sophisticated levels of search capability cannot alleviate the problems caused by inconsistencies or omissions of useful data in constructing and maintaining indexes.

Quality of information access in online catalogs cannot be determined just by looking at the total number of access points. Many factors determine quality, including record content and structure, added entry indexing, length of field-derived data (number of characters), stopword lists, treatment of punctuation, and indexing of descriptive data from bibliographical records. Powerful, flexible, and convenient access is possible through the use of sophisticated online capabilities such as searching on truncated words and phrases, use of question marks as wild cards for characters and works, keyword searching aided by the use of Boolean or word proximity operators, and limiting search results by date, format, and language. Being able to select the formats and arrangement of results to be displayed or printed also advances the user beyond other forms of catalog access in terms of flexibility and convenience of use.

Going back to the title of this paper, I strongly believe that the online catalog is certainly a friend of both the user and the librarian. As I observe the use of the MSUS/PASL online catalog and talk to librarians about the online catalog, this belief is continually reinforced. In fact, I know several reference librarians who have stated that a condition of employment for any future job change will be the availability of a current generation online catalog.

The major advantage of the online catalog (among many positive advantages and no significant disadvantages) is that it permits a global approach to information access and retrieval and hence reference and research work. The entire library collection becomes a "reference collection" because of the ability of the computer to utilize all of the bibliographic and descriptive information in the MARC record. For example, form subdivisions, such as bibliography, indexes, abstracts, periodicals, handbooks, etc., can be exploited to produce definitive lists of information resources by subject and format. The use of cataloging conventions and uniform titles, such as works, piano, selections, thesis, etc., can be exploited to obtain specific types of material. The use of thematic indexing, such as the BWV or Schmieder number for the individual works of Bach, can be exploited to obtain specific items very quickly. The use of descriptive terms, such as D major, can be used to obtain items designed for a specific application.

Another example of exploiting the content of the bibliographic record is use of notes, such as the extensive notation of where an item is indexed which is given in most serial records. The use of format, date, and language limiters is yet another example of using data from the MARC record (these limiters may also be expanded to include geographic, publisher, and other production and content factors).

The ability to find information in the online catalog is only limited by the creative perspective of the user. However, a knowledge of the structure and content of the computer or MARC bibliographic record and of how the computer processes commands is very useful in applying this creativity. One significant difference from the use of the card catalog is that the user of an online catalog does not need to know rules, but can instead think from a logical relationship and concept point of view about what he or she needs as a result of the information access and retrieval process.

Another example of a way to make the online catalog work for the user to speed up the information access and retrieval process is to store some types of searches which have universal application. For example, a reference librarian at Mankato State University has a set of searches which he carries out and stores for future access each time that he begins work at the reference desk. One that he does, because a frequently asked question is for a list of reference works on a topic or a list of periodicals on a topic, is to do a subject term search under several of the subject form subdivisions previously mentioned. The storage of these sets of responses enables him to quickly produce a listing when a student asks for periodicals about biology, that is, he does a term search on biology and then and then (using the Boolean operator "and") limits the results of the search by the previously saved set which resulted from the subject term search on periodicals.

The online catalog offers the user both expanded and more convenient access to information, and provides functional capabilities, even in the simpler implementations, far more diverse and powerful than those of any other form of catalog. Charles Hildreth (1982) states "The online catalog is not merely a flashy electronic card or book catalog, fashioned in someone's Rube Goldberg-like fantasy, having the same access and display capabilities for unit records that just happen to be stored in a highly reduced form in a foreign, coded, machine-readable language." We are indeed in a new world of information access and retrieval that is rapidly changing and will continue to change the future.

References

Bausser, Jaye. 1981. "Online Catalogs." *RTSD Newsletter* 6 (July/August):43-44.

Hildreth, Charles R. 1982. *Online Public Access Catalogs: The User Interface*. Dublin, Ohio: OCLC.

Lawrence, Gary S. 1985. "System Features for Subject Access in the Online Catalog." *Library Resources and Technical Services* 29 (January/March):16-33.

Penhale, Sara J., and Nancy Taylor. 1968. "Integrating End-User Searching into a Bibliographic Instruction Program." *RQ* 27 (Winter):212-20.

Shaw, Ward. 1986. "Aristotle Meets Plato in the Library Catalog." Unpublished paper, May.

Stefik, Mark. 1986. "The Next Knowledge Medium." *AI Magazine* 6:(Spring):40-42.

Staffing the New Technology Reference Desk

KATHLEEN PRENDERGAST
Manager, Information Services
Northwestern University
Cranston, Illinois

In any operation management must account for two components: the workers and the tools. In both libraries and in corporations the past does not bode well for the future.

Equipment that could increase the productivity of white-collar employees is not being purchased and employees whose use of such equipment could enhance the services delivered to clients are not being trained.

> The tendency to automate only the routine aspects of business is also evident in the difference between corporate investment in tools for blue- and white-collar workers. In the 1970's expenditures averaged $25,000 for blue-collar workers as compared with $2000 for each white-collar worker. This disparity is, in turn, reflected in productivity growth rates in recent years. Blue-collar productivity has grown (albeit slowly), but white-collar productivity has declined. It is safe to predict that white-collar productivity will continue to lag behind that of blue-collar workers until and unless business applies the same management

> techniques to information that it uses in other areas. (Diebold 1985, 40).

A survey of 322 senior human resource directors from *Fortune* 1500 companies reported that 12,000,000 American employees are now obsolete.

> Three fourths of the personnel directors reported that their employees wanted retraining. But the survey found that only 36 percent of those large corporations retrained their experienced engineers or technical people or middle managers. Instead, the majority either hired new employees to replace the obsolete ones, put them in jobs that required no skills, or just got rid of them. (Bardwick 1986 140).

Despite the endorsement by the RASD Standards Committee of continuing education, we all know that we are behind the eight ball in bringing staff up to speed. What is needed in high-technology reference desk staffing is a planning process similar to that applied to major automation projects.

> The planning process--crucial to the success of any automation project--should not only establish a path for making the many decisions inherent in specifying and selecting the most desirable system, but also prepare the library for the system's acceptance implementation. In short, the planning process should facilitate both decision-making and organization change. (Drabenstott 1985, 15)

In an organization that planned for the use of advanced technology at the reference desk, employees would be encouraged to experiment with, for example, new databases. Taped to the online terminal at your reference desk could be a list of vendors' monthly promotions. One of the most wasteful practices of too many online coordinators and reference managers is their hoarding of free resources such as Dow Jones's monthly 30-minute practice times on a variety of files, or DIALOG's special monthly discounts, usually advertised in *Chronolog*.

One red herring that is apparently a problem for many librarians but hardly a crisis for this one is the fact that machines require tending. Mendelsohn (1985, 182) reports that: "An example of role conflict is illustrated by a situation in which a highly trained reference specialist has to spend a great deal of time with patrons working on complex reference problems while simultaneously performing clerical duties such as changing copy machine paper and making change."

Because new technologies are invariably fraught with mechanical problems, the planning process for new technology should consider the burden on librarians of technical malfunctions. More than one search center and reference desk has assigned one librarian as the in-house expert on systems and equipment. The reference manager may then set up a buddy system to pair that expert with a neophyte, and slowly develop staff-wide expertise.

My point today is that staff must be involved in reference service planning if organizational change in response to new technology is to result in better service to our patrons.

Too many reference staff concentrate on sincerity when a systematic approach to achieving accuracy would be more appropriate. A problem with new technology at our reference desks today is that sincere technocrats are exercising influence that I believe is negatively affecting our service delivery. Too many veterans with extensive knowledge of collections are being co-opted by technologically sophisticated but bibliographically naive and educationally deficient newcomers.

The challenge of reference management is to instill in the veteran an appreciation for the appropriate application of technology while educating librarians in collection appreciation.

Based on my unscientific, but sincerely held views and first-hand experience at academic, public, and special library reference desks for more than a decade, I believe that two elements characterize the successfully staffed reference desk. First, a strong, consistent manager who provides staff with a realistic, unambiguous, and flexible service philosophy. Second, a continuing process of staff training, experimentation, and evaluation that engages reference staff in the process of service delivery.

The process of reference desk staffing begins with bilateral creditability. Does the reference manager have enough factual information about the operation of the desk to assign and schedule appropriate staff? Do employees agree with their manager's assessment of staff resource requirements?

Hiring new employees may involve testing. Interviewing library science graduates for an entry-level position, everyone expects computer and online experience; someone should include a reference component. Looking for a reference librarian to handle business clipping responsibilities, I once asked new library science graduates to mention any two articles about business they had read recently in *any* paper or magazine. Only three of the 10 applicants could recall a single article!

Brown found that "there is some relationship between answer format and sources used, so that one expects a request for a document to lead to the card catalog; for a short answer, to the ready reference collection; and for gathered information to the general reference or circulating collections" (Brown 1985, 299).

She concludes that "The fact that two-thirds of all questions recorded were of an informational nature and that only nine percent of all questions resulted in a search of either the general reference or circulating collections that most questions can be answered by well-trained paraprofessionals staff" (Brown 1985, 300).

There is no reason why reference managers cannot use properly trained paraprofessionals on a reference desk. The question is how and when? One can begin by looking at the categories of questions received at the desk.

Seattle Public Library schedules a paraprofessional from 1 to 9 P.M. daily for stock quotes. Between 9 and 1 P.M., patrons are directed to the stock quotation reference area if they want to do the research themselves. That stock quote service, with hours, is posted in the phone book.

Chicago Public Library uses a paraprofessional for some telephone requests for online searches. The search strategy and results are reviewed by a librarian before the client sees them.

In reference practice, judgment is expressed in how one answers such question as "Where is the *Wall Street Journal* located?" or "What is the current Consumer Price Index?" Any experienced public librarian knows that the first answer is not "down the hall and take a right at the index table." Judgment requires that we ask our patrons (and train our staff to ask our patrons) if they are looking for stock quotations or articles about companies or business subjects. Often, they really want the *Daily Stock Price Index*, or the *Capital Changes Reporter*. Similarly, it is not a bad idea to ask the person needing the consumer price index if their question is in relation to a salary increase. Whether employee or employer, it may be useful for that client to know of the Producer Price Index, the American Chamber of Commerce Association's Comparative Cost-of-Living Indexes, possibly even the *Places Rated Almanac*.

We are exercising judgement when we select a source and management should look for ways to encourage reference staff to do just that. Whether the source is online or a book should not be the deciding factor.

Terence Crowley, reviewing major studies of unobtrusive reference tests, suggests that researchers may produce information useful to working librarians by deducing question difficulty rather than inducing it. Look at the questions we can answer correctly, then inspect specific questions with which we have difficulty.

"By reporting the data in terms of sets of questions that represent varying degrees of experienced difficulty, researchers will enable librarians to test and compare themselves to whatever peer groups seem appropriate" (Crowley 1985).

Technology gives us the tools to engage in useful self-examination of the type recommended by Crowley. At the InfoCenter, the Chicago Public Library's quick answer telephone reference department, a NEXIS terminal was installed in 1985. For the first two months of its installation, we reviewed the paper record of all searches done by librarians. The purpose of our review was to ascertain that librarians had been properly trained to search the system efficiently.

"Attention must turn away from evaluating reference service to evaluating the performance of the reference librarian in relation to this or her primary function" (Young 1984, 127).

To examine the effectiveness of our service delivery, we must be ready to evaluate the librarians and other desk staff for reference skills.

> Points to consider in such an evaluation should be consistent and specific, for example: an awareness of new reference titles, a

> knowledge of those bibliographies providing control over the documents collection, reference technique capability, that is, the ability to find sources which will successfully meet information needs, courtesy and patience in dealing with patrons, a demeanor or attitude which encourages patrons to approach the reference desk, etc. (Young 1984, 127)

Peer review is a great idea, but it is a difficult process to establish. I believe it is worth the effort because I believe librarianship is a collegial endeavor. There is no good reason why employees should engage in peer review unless they see some benefits to themselves. In a busy online search center, we asked searchers to review each other's search forms, which contained the original patron question and the strategy worked out by the librarian. This was found to be useful, as it gave the searchers new ideas and encouraged them to discuss search strategies among themselves.

Let me conclude with a list of some short term goals and the mechanisms that I've seen used effectively to meet those goals.

GOAL: Encourage employees' use of online tools

MECHANISM: Shield cost from staff, downplay the annual online budget until staff is regularly searching. Encourage use of training files.

GOAL: Educate staff on online reference.

MECHANISM: Route *Chronolog* and blue sheets to all reference desk staff or keep at desk; post free online time, run half hour workshops with invited salesperson from database suppliers.

GOAL: Introduce new technology.

MECHANISM: Assign one employee as project director. Don't be afraid to give project to someone who has been antitechnology. Part of job description must be 1) fix machines; 2) buddy system with other employees; and 3) continuing education. TAKE AT LEAST ONE CURRENT

JOB AWAY FROM DESIGNATED PROJECT DIRECTOR.

GOAL: Train staff in continuing technologies.

MECHANISM: Budget for training (not just for travel, not just for administrators and certainly not just for librarians).

GOAL: Require productive conference/workshop attendance.

MECHANISM: Require employees to share reports on conference minutes, materials, etc.

GOAL: Develop staff skills in broad subject areas.

MECHANISM: Approve employee attendance at local non-library-related conferences. We've approved attendance at Council on Foreign Relations meetings, Chicago Women in Business, local women's history groups, high school competitions (where librarians serve as judges), science fairs, etc.

GOAL: Provide staff with same services you provide patrons.

MECHANISM: Route materials around to each other on all sorts of topics. Northwestern University Library, for example, has an SDI service for staff, at 10¢ a page; I get 25 tables of contents.

GOAL: Protect staff from nonproductive work.

MECHANISM: Cultivate leadership in your department: delegate lower-level staff to attend administrative meetings.

GOAL: Don't try to "level-out" staff; "stroke" the individual talents of employees.

MECHANISM: For example, assign stock quote bibliography to an employee who trades in the market.

GOAL: Continually reinforce in staff the usefulness of library research.

MECHANISM: Provide staff with free online searches on consumer product evaluations at Christmas.

Julie Neway (1985, 159) has recently described the role of the librarian in a way I find useful when considering reference staff: An ability to organize data and information for people to use; an awareness of the totality of information resources and the strategies (that is, probabilities of success) in searching for information in any specific situation; an awareness of, and capability in, the range of information, technologies--from print to computers--a sensitivity to use, uses and users of information, allowing the profession to consider the human context in the design of systems and services; and a strong tradition of service that demands attention be paid to client satisfaction.

A commitment by reference managers to share the excitement of effective high-technology service delivery will, I believe, increase our ability to both satisfy our clients and keep good staff.

References

Bardwick, Judith M. 1986. *The Plateauing Trap: How to Avoid It in Your Career . . . and Your Life*. New York: AMACOM.

Brown, Diane M. 1985. "Telephone Reference Questions: A Characterization by Subject Answer Format, and Level of Complexity." *RQ* 24, no. 39 (Spring):290-303.

Crowley, Terence. 1985. *Managing Information: The Challenge and the Opportunity*. New York: AMACOM.

Drabenstott, Jon. 1985. "Automation Planning and Organizational Change: A Functional Model for Developing a Systems Plan." *Library Hi Tech* 3, no. 3:15-24.

Mendelsohn, Henry N. 1985. "Role Conflict and Ambiguity in Reference Librarianship." *Reference Librarian,* no 12 (Spring/Summer):179-86.

Neway, Julie M. 1985. *The Information Specialist as a Team Player in the Research Process.* New Directions in Librarianship, no. 9. Conn.: Greenwood Press.

RASD ALA Standards Committee. 1979. *A Commitment to Information Services Developments Guidelines.*

Young, William F. 1984. "Evaluating the Reference Librarian." *Reference Librarian,* no. 11 (Fall/Winter):123-29.

Part 3
The Library Catalog, Automated Systems, and Human Interaction

The Vanishing Library Catalog: Access, Bibliography, and Technology

MICHAEL K. BUCKLAND
Assistant Vice President
for Library Plans and Policies
University of California System
Berkeley, California

The year 1987 is twenty years after Samuel Lazerow became chairman of the US National Libraries Taskforce on Automation and fifteen years since he retired from Federal service and went to work in the quite different environment of the Institute for Scientific Information. It seems appropriate, therefore, to take the opportunity of the Samuel Lazerow Lecture for 1987 to consider the opportunities and challenge of changing technology, especially as that is the theme of the conference at which this lecture is presented.

The stated intention of the organizers of this Lazerow lecture was that the lecture should provoke. An effective way to provoke is to raise basic questions concerning some matter that is central and accepted in orthodox opinion. The invitation to present this Lazerow lecture coincided with some reconsideration of the central and accepted role of the library catalog.

The library catalog has had various forms: traditionally in bookform; for several decades primarily in cardform; occasionally in microform; and recently online. Regardless of the technological form, the historic role of the catalog is central:

1. A library's catalog is the key to the collections.

2. Cataloging is a central feature of librarianship, of "assembling, preserving, and making available for use the records of human experience" in the rolling rhetoric of Shera.[1]

3. Online catalogs are the hottest topic in library technology at this time.

4. For library users, the new online library catalogs are the most popular development since photocopying machines were introduced.

It would be highly unorthodox to suggest that the centrality of the library catalog and the development of online catalogs might be obsolescent, even an aberration. Yet, in the long view, if one re-examines basic assumptions, considers long-term changes in library technology, and holds to the need to provide effective and efficient library service, a case can be made that prevailing assumptions concerning catalogs are questionable.

Some disclaimers are in order. These remarks concentrate on long term strategic questions, not on short term tactical and operational issues. Nobody should be discouraged from developing their catalog or from seeking to provide online access to catalog records. At best what follows may be relevant to how the library catalog may evolve in the longer term.

In considering the future of libraries and of the technologies at our disposal, one change seems of particular significance. This is the shift in the nature of library materials from paper and microform to paper and microform and databases. (The term *database* is used here to refer generically to materials in machine-readable form, whether text, numerical data, or images). The interesting question is not the future of the book on paper, but, rather, the implications of library materials becoming available in machine-readable form in addition to paper and microform media.

Libraries are concerned with knowledge, information, facts, and beliefs.[2] The purpose of a library, in the words of Frederick Kilgour, "is to actively participate in the evolution of those profoundly human creations: beauty, filth, justice, and knowledge."[3] As a practical matter, however, libraries deal with physical objects, with representations of knowledge, information, facts, and beliefs. Libraries deal with text and images, or, more strictly, with text-bearing objects and image-bearing objects, with millions and millions of these objects on miles and miles of shelving. It would be reasonable to suppose, therefore, that any significant change in the nature or characteristics of these physical objects could well have profound consequences for library operations.

It is in this context that almost every aspect of orthodox opinion concerning library catalogs becomes suspect. The reconsideration of orthodox opinions should not be seen as negative, since, even if it were established that the orthodoxy of cataloging was headed in the wrong direction, that very conclusion implies that some other, unorthodox alternative exists that would point in some other, better direction.

The normal method for trying to foresee future developments is to take the status quo as a point of departure and to contemplate the probable impact current trends and of new information technologies. In this case the reverse is suggested: Taking new information technologies for granted and contemplating the effects of old information technology. hindsight, after all, is said to be more accurate than foresight. What then would hindsight tell us? What would constitute a conservative critique of library catalogs? It should be stressed that we should not be concerned merely with card catalogs, but with library catalogs generally in whatever form.

The first observation from hindsight in relation to the unquestionably exciting contemporary catalog scene is that we have been there before. The excitement in the 1970s and 1980s over the application of new techniques to new improved online catalog access to library collections is, in a significant sense, a replay of the excitement over the application of new techniques to improve catalog access to library collections in the 1870s and 1880s. At that time, when modern librarianship was defined, the traditional author-ordered finding list style of library catalog, pioneered in the

Bodleian Library catalog of 1620, no longer seemed sufficient. What librarians wanted to provide was enhanced access to the works in the collection. Under the leadership of Pannizzi, Cutter, Dewey, and others, a revolution in catalog technique was achieved. In essence, a superstructure of bibliographical apparatus was built on top of basic library records in order to achieve sophisticated access: Complex, precoordinated subject headings (such as Library of Congress Subject Headings); Authority control to standardize headings; Syndetic structure of preferred headings, authority control, and cross-references (both "See . . . and "See Also . . ."); Title entry in addition to author and subject entries; Dictionary arrangement; Systematic classification schemes combined with Cutter numbers for relative shelf location; and the move to use cardboard as the technology of choice.

Those years were clearly exciting times. However, they differed in a significant way from the present transformation of library catalogs: Users did not entirely appreciate the new "hi-tech" library catalogs. Indeed, there was a vigorous debate between the exponents of better library catalogs and others (usually bibliographers and library users) who argued that the subject approach to literatures could be handled only through bibliographies and that the construction of elaborate library catalogs would be an obstacle to the compilation of the bibliographies that were needed. The debate has been well summarized by Swank.[4]

Proponents of bibliographies argued that bibliographies could be:

- More complete than catalogs, because they extend beyond a single library's collections
- More selective, focussing on the interests of a specific clientele and, therefore, of higher "precision" in the terminology of information retrieval theory
- More capable of special arrangements, as opposed to standardized universal schemes of classification and of subject description
- More flexible, because each new bibliography can be done differently

- More detailed, indicating individual papers within periodicals and conference proceedings
- More easily deployed to cover new topics of interest as needed
- More cost effective, because, unlike a card catalog, copies of a bibliography can be placed in many libraries
- More competently compiled, because bibliographers are more likely than catalogers to be expert subject specialists
- More coherent, because bibliographers begin with a topical perspective and select references for it whereas catalogers must cope with an influx of individual documents to be sorted

These and other assertions were rebutted by catalogers who argued, for example, that an individual library user was primarily concerned with the contents of the local library, that a single comprehensive approach provided a broader view, that cataloging codes did permit the making of analytical entries for individual papers,[5] and so on.

Library administrators knew that libraries had to have some form of catalog and, overall, catalogers had their way. It was not that bibliography disappeared but rather that it moved outside of the mainstream of librarianship. Defining bibliography as the making of lists and of indexes to lists,[6] a library catalog is, in effect, a form of bibliography defined as the intersection of two sets: Objects that are held in a specific library and are listed above a certain level of description, effectively titles of periodicals and editions of monographs. Yet catalogs came increasingly to be seen as separate and apart form bibliography. Reference librarians would continue to compile bibliographies, often on their own time, but much of the activity developed outside the mainstream of librarianship: by individual scholars, by professional and scholarly societies, by "documentalists" and "special librarians," by private firms (e.g., Bowker, Wilson, Lockheed), and , especially in the U.S. after World War II, by government agencies (e.g., NTIS, ERIC).

Shera commented disapprovingly on "The librarians retreat from bibliography."[7] Swank[8] struggled to find ways of achieving the best of both worlds, of the administrative necessity of catalogs and the advantages of subject-specialized bibliographies, but in the last resort he was not successful. One explanation of why he was not successful is technological, that integration is not practical given the technology of paper and of cardboard. One can keep rearranging card catalogs in new ways, but it is not practical to do so. It is possible to insert entries from bibliographies into card catalogs, but that, too, is not very practical.

In terms of hindsight, how would this be seen if we were to take for granted the new technology of computers, especially mass storage, online services, and telecommunications, to explore the possibilities and limitations of past technology. It is difficult, in practice, to analyze objectively that which is familiar. What one needs is the proverbial Man from Mars. An extraterrestrial with sufficient technology to visit Earth would probably find our contemporary computer technology rather clumsy and comment on the inadequate use of standards and protocols. Perhaps an extraterrestrial would be more intrigued by the properties of an information technology that might not exist on a planet without vegetation and is certainly different from computer technology: paper. The extraterrestrial might observe that paper is energy-efficient, requiring light to be read by, but no electricity and that paper is effective in a wide range of environmental conditions.

However, paper and cardboard have two other properties that differentiate them even more markedly from computer technology:

1. Paper is a strictly localized information technology. Unlike computer technology the paper and the would-be reader have to be in the same place. If they are not, the one or the other has to move. This may sound trivial but its effects are not. Some years ago at a large midwestern campus there were twelve subscriptions to *Chemical Abstracts*. It was felt by some to be rather extravagant to have so many subscriptions, but no group of users was willing to give up its own subscription and have to walk part way across the campus to use some other

subscription. It required the personal attention of the university president to achieve a reduction in subscriptions. The moral is that the localized nature of paper (and, it would seem, of library users) is a powerful factor. In this, paper as an information technology differs from computers as an information technology. How many users of the Lockheed Dialog service or of Compuserve know where the information is stored? Does it matter whether they know or not?

2. Paper is also an isolated technology. Books lend themselves to use by only one person at a time. In this a book is more like a telescope than a television. Again this differs radically from computer technology. When using an online catalog one does not ordinarily even know how many other people, if any, are using the catalog at the same time.

Microform would presumably be viewed by the extraterrestrial as paper with bad habits: It is even more local in that a reading machine must also be in the same place; again it is suited for use by only one person at a time; and one cannot even scribble on it.

The property of "localness" that paper has is highly relevant to our view of catalogs. Since paper is so "localized," it is very important to have a guide to local collections and that is precisely the traditional purpose of a library catalog. For material in a medium that does not have this property of "localness," however, it does not matter where it is stored. What matters is only that a copy of it is conveniently locally *accessible*, a virtual copy on the glowing screen of a terminal, perhaps, or an electronic transfer of the text to a local equipment. What is needed for such material is not a traditional library catalog but rather a union catalog of material in several places or, better, a bibliography that also includes an indication of where and how a copy can be obtained. Reliance on a catalog providing access only to what is locally stored as opposed to what is locally accessible would be irrelevant, unhelpful, even perverse.

A story is told of scientific management experts who were sent to improve the efficiency of the British army on the Western front during the First World War. Doing "time and motion" analyses of gun emplacements they noticed that the soldiers were trained to stand with both hands held vertically upright above their right shoulders at the time the gun was fired. No one knew why this was done. It would have seemed more sensible for them to put their hands over their ears to muffle the noise. On investigation it was established that they were trained to hold horses' heads to calm them at the time of the explosion. In the meanwhile the use of horses had been discontinued, but the military drill had not yet been changed. The moral is that thought and action do not always keep pace with technological change.

Could it be that in librarianship there are examples of calming the horses after the horses have gone? In 1983 there was a conference with the promising title *Online Catalogs, Online References: Converging Trends*.[9] Since catalog records and reference records are both forms of bibliographical record, with similar contents and structure, searched with similar software in similar ways, and since both tend to use the same sorts of computer, one might have expected some fruitful ideas about convergence. Perusal of the published proceeding reveals but three sentences indicating awareness of the possibility of convergence. It is as if the constraints imposed by the technology of paper and of cardboard were still determining the conceptual view, even though paper and cardboard had ceased to be the technology of choice for both cataloging and reference a decade earlier and the very title of the conference specified by the word "online" a focus on a technology that has properties clearly different from that of the superseded technology of paper and cardboard.

The traditional catalog can be viewed as a technological response to the difficulty of combining bibliographies and library records. Bibliographical apparatus is needed to help the library user find out what exists and, sometimes, to help clarify the identity of what is known to exist. Records of local holdings are needed to locate copies of the texts once they have been identified. Both are needed and they need to be used in conjunction, but, as Swank found, bibliographies and library records do not combine well so long as paper and of cardboard, what happens to the validity of the design when this technology is no longer being used and its limitations irrelevant?

Let us consider the catalog of a university chemistry library. A conventional catalog would list the titles of journals and editions of monographs, but it is clear that this fails to provide bibliographical access to the literature of most interest to the users of the library, who are primarily interested in a finer level, such as articles in journals and papers in conference proceedings. An orthodox cataloger might respond that the traditional catalog is clearly inadequate and that the catalog should be enriched to contain entries for individual articles and papers. A bibliographer might respond that the incompleteness of coverage in the catalog was so severe that users should concentrate on bibliographies such as *Chemical Abstracts* and wish that the bibliographies could be made to indicate local holdings. In a post-cardboard age, with machine-readable bibliographies and computerized library records, there are imaginable ways in which records in bibliographies could be linked via, for example, ISSN or other unique identifying numbers, to library holdings records.[11] To the extent that this could be done, it would appear that the traditional catalog would not be needed any more and will have been superseded.

A doctoral student once set out to expunge from his mind the influences of catalog cards and to imagine catalog rules for an online world. He did not achieve this goal. One explanation is that in an online world the customary notion of a library catalog disappears or, more accurately, it changes and diminishes. Fantasize a library user using a library in an online world. First the catalog would be searched and one or more catalog records retrieved. The user might reasonably want next to examine the table of contents of a title. In an online world, the table of contents would also be online so displaying it would be a matter of pressing the appropriate key. Next the user might want to look for specific terms or names in the index of the book, which, also, of course, would be available online and could lead to specific patches of text, which, in turn, would be online. If that were not enough, one could reasonably expect that, with the text available in machine-readable form, there would be a full concordance available of all words used in the text. At this point the user might decide to abandon that particular text and go back to the catalog records to identify another text or else scan the subject headings with a view to reformulating the search. One would expect a continual changing from broad view to focus on details. The system would need to have what Manfred Kochen has described, by analogy with a camera lens, as "zoomability" [12]. It is not that the data elements familiar to us as catalog records would have disappeared, but rather the catalog would cease to exist as a separate entity. Instead, the catalog data would be a subset of a much broader set of data elements and the catalog function would have become one feature in a suite of related functions in online library use.

In summary, it is clear that as we move away from the limitations of the technology of paper and of cardboard and into an online environment the relationships of the catalog to other entities is significantly changed: the user no longer has to go to the catalog; the catalog ceases to be separated from the items cataloged; the catalog should no longer be defined in terms of local holdings; and the technological basis for separating the catalog from other aspects of bibliography is no longer present. Cumulatively, these conclusions leave little in place of the catalog as we are accustomed to it.

It is sometimes prudent to retreat to basic principles. The following are suggested:

1. Making documents available necessitates local holdings records of each library's collections. Holdings statements are what give access to the texts or images sought by providing the call number, which is also the basis for ascertaining the availability status of the document and for sending a message, electronic or otherwise, to request delivery of the original, of a photocopy, of a telefacsimile, or, in the future, access to a machine-readable version.

2. So far as library users are concerned, however, "local holdings" needs to be redefined as "locally accessible". So long as libraries were concerned with text on paper, on microform, on clay tablets, or on any other media characterized by localness, "local holdings" (to the extent cataloged and available) *were* what was locally accessible.

As machine-readable resources are also made available these two terms cease to be synonymous and what is locally accessible becomes larger and, therefore, more important than what is locally held.

3. Library users need bibliographies to identify what is wanted.

4. Bibliographical records need to be related to records of what is locally accessible in order to gain access to the texts or images identified as wanted.

If these four conditions can be met, then it is not clear that a role for the library catalog, as we currently know it, remains. There are other uses for hand when there are no longer horses to be calmed. There are other needs for scarce library resources if the rationale for the traditional library catalog were to vanish. We should explore the possibilities of automation and be willing to work on unconventional techniques, following the example of Samuel Lazerow.

Notes

1. J. H. Shera. *The Foundations of Education of Librarianship* (New York: Becker & Hayes, 1972), 185.

2. D. Bergen. *Issues of Access in the New Information Age* Kingston: University of Rhode Island, 1984. (ERIC Report ED 271119).

3. F. G. Kilgour. "The Impact of Technology on Libraries," *The Information Society: Issues and Answers*, ed. E. J. Josey (Phoenix, Ariz.: Oryx Press, 1978), 12-19. Reprinted in F. G. Kilgour, *Collected Papers of Frederick G. Kilgour: OCLC Years* (Dublin, Ohio: OCLC, 1984), 393-97.

4. R. C. Swank. "Subject Catalogs, Classifications, or Bibliographies? A Review of Critical Discussions, 1876-1942," *Library Quarterly* 14 (1944):316-32. Reprinted in R. C. Swank, *A Unifying Influence: Essays* (Metuchen, N.J.: Scarecrow Press, 1981), 1-27.

5. For two examples of library catalogs with copious entries for individual papers see the *Index-Catalog of the Library of the Surgeon General's Office, United States Army*, 1880, and the *Catalogue of the Library of the Peabody Institute of the City of Baltimore*, 1883-92.

6. P. G. Wilson. *Two Kinds of Power: An Essay on Bibliographical Control* (Berkeley.: University of California Press, 1968).

7. J. H. Shera. *The Foundations of Education for Librarianship* (New York: Becker & Hayes, 1972), 185-90.

8. For example, R. C. Swank. "Subject Cataloging in the Subject-Departmentalized Library," in *Bibliographical Organization*, ed. J. H. Shera and M. Egan (Chicago: Chicago University Press, 1951), 187-99. Reprinted in R. C. Swank, *A Unifying Influence: Essays* (Metuchen, N.J.: Scarecrow Press, 1981), 171-90.

9. *Online Catalogs, Online Reference: Converging Trends. Proceedings of a Library and Information Technology Association Preconference Institute, 1983, Los Angeles*, ed. B. Aveney and B. Butler, 1-2 (B. Butler) and 155 (M. Gorman).

10. In terms of the MARC communications format one might state that, in general, fields before field 900 are bibliographical and pertain to the title and fields 900 and above are local and pertain to the copy.

11. The Division of Library Automation, Office of the President, University of California is mounting part of the MEDLINE database in conjunction with the University's online union library catalog, with support from the National Library of Medicine (Grant #G08LM04466-01). A experimental linking of MEDLINE bibliographical records with library catalog holdings records is expected as part of this project.

12. M. Kochen. "Directory Design for Networks of Information and Referral Centers," *Library Quarterly* 42 (1972):59-76.

Current Uses of Automated Systems: A Review and Status Report

RICHARD W. BOSS
Consultant
Information Systems Consultants, Inc.
Washington, D.C.

Local library systems are being used differently today than they were as recently as three years ago. We have moved away from an emphasis on circulation to multifunction, integrated systems capable of supporting acquisitions, serials control, circulation, and patron access catalog modules. Three years ago over 85 percent of all installed systems had only circulation fully implemented. The typical system was a staff tool: selected by and for staff. Today, more than 50 percent of all systems purchased in the past three years have a patron access catalog implemented. When circulation is also operational, the patron access catalog provides access not only to holdings information, but also to availability information. In the future--as acquisitions and serials control are also widely implemented--the patron will have a window on all of the files of the library through the patron access catalog: on order, in process, at bindery, in circulation, etc. This will make a local library system first and foremost a tool for patrons. This will be particularly true in libraries with low circulation volumes for which greater throughput at the circulation desk is not a high priority.

The transition from staff to patron tool increases the importance of full bibliographic records, authority control, full integration of all modules, and user interfaces. While patrons may not want to display full bibliographic records, keyword searching and qualification by year, language, format, etc. will require far more data elements than circulation applications. Quality control will be even more important than in the past, with good authority control, including the ability to make global changes in headings with a single machine action. It will be essential that patrons can determine whether a particular issue of a journal has been checked in--periodic transfer of summary information from the serials control module won't do. The extremes of expert and novice modes will have to be augmented with intermediate modes.

The transition to the local library system as a patron tool may increase the importance of PCs as workstations. We have been using PCs for several years at circulation to collect charges and discharges when the host system is down. The potential is even greater for patrons. Were some of the so-called "dumb" terminals replaced with PC-based work-stations, patrons could download search results and manipulate them with a text editing or word processing package, thus incorporating bibliographic information into manuscripts. Given a gateway through the CPU (central processing unit), they could access remote databases. Searching aids could be provided on the PC. One hopes that we will move to post processing capability: the use of search results from one search to formulate another search. For example, the results of a remote bibliographic database search could be downloaded and run against the local database to determine which of the citations can be found in the local collection.

As patrons become accustomed to using the local library system within the library, they will probably begin to demand remote access from home and office. In most cases that will mean the availability of dial-in ports. In some cases it will mean interfacing the local library system with a LAN (local area network). Patrons may also press for access to other library systems to look for materials not found in the local database. While librarians may be able to use terminal-to-computer interfaces successfully, patrons will need computer-to-computer interfaces which are transparent--that is, there is no need for the terminal user to know the commands and other unique requirements of the other system. The Open System Interconnection (OSI) Reference Model constitutes a set of standards which will permit heterogeneous or incompatible computer systems to link with one another without requiring special skills of terminal operators. The standards will be usable over LANs within a few miles, over the metropolitan area networks local telephone companies are now beginning to support, or over nationwide telephone circuits.

As patrons become more sophisticated in their use of local library systems, they may begin to demand more than bibliographic information. There is no technological reason why journal citation files cannot be retrieved through local library systems. The major requirements are the development of loader programs, minor modification in the patron access catalog software, and more economical storage devices. Several local library system vendors have already developed loader programs (usually at a cost of no more than $2,000 per file source) and improved searching software. To date all require the use of magnetic storage media, but there is a reasonable prospect that optical digital disk storage devices will become available from local library system vendors in the next three years. That might make it possible to load large files like MEDLINE or ERIC on a single optical digital disk, with access from all patron access catalog terminals. This might be more cost *and* service effective than supporting journal citation databases locally on CDROM drives attached to PCs. In the longer term, image databases might also be controlled through the local library system. An image database might be images of pages of backfiles of journals on optical digital disk, or images of slides, photographs or other nonprint materials.

It is unrealistic for any one library to pursue these developments on its own. The key to the future for a library interested in the scenario I have sought to describe is finding a vendor which has the human and financial resources, and the interest, to pursue the implications of the transition of the local library system from staff tool to patron tool. While vendors tend to be conservative about making commitments beyond the four major modules (acquisitions, serials control, circulation, and patron access catalog), as more libraries express their interest in future development beyond the core modules, responsiveness is increasing. Several vendors are now signing contracts calling for OSI conformity and journal citation support on magnetic media; and are pursuing research in optical digital disk technology.

People and Technology: A Delicate Balance

WAYNE A. WIEGAND
Associate Professor
School of Library and Information Science
University of Wisconsin
Madison, Wisconsin

It was with some serious reservations that I ultimately decided several weeks ago to accept Al Trezza's invitation to address this conference. When he called in early February, he proudly ran down the list of names of all of the heavy-hitters in the profession who would be addressing the opportunities and challenges likely to confront us over the coming years by our changing technology. And the list is certainly impressive--Bill Welsh, JoAn Segal, Mary Ellen Jacob, Vivian Arterbury, Mike Buckland, and Richard Boss, to name only a few. My assignment, Al said, was to return the conference to thinking about the human being, to reminding us that there *is* a delicate balance between the people we want to serve and the changing technology that makes the prospects of our professional future so exciting. Nice assignment, I said to myself. The big names project a rosy future; an airhead like me is supposed to bring us back to the reality of the present. And an old German saying kept flashing through my mind--the dogs always nip at the heels of the last person in line. Like I say--I had some serious reservations about accepting Al's invitation, but here I am.

In part because the invitation gives me a unique opportunity to share with an audience of professionals--a group of people on the firing line every day--some of the thoughts I have gathered from recent reading in the social sciences and the humanities which I think reflect directly on what we have been learning over the past few days. But before I share these thoughts, I want to establish very clearly that I am not a Luddite; I don't want to destroy the machinery, nor do I wish to stay the momentum of its development. And please, PLEASE, don't take my computer away from me. I fully agree with all previous speakers who cite the need to prepare for a set of futures based upon our perceptions of the direction in which changing technology will take us. We are indeed fortunate to have such bright people leading our profession; it augurs well for our own professional future, and I fully encourage these people to keep thinking, to keep addressing us, to keep preparing us for that future.

But we also have to be aware that we work within limits, limits imposed upon us not only by the technology, but also by the human mind, its ability to process the very information we seek to acquire, store, and sometimes retrieve, and its unique power to select from a vast universe only those bits of information it finds useful in making sense of the world. It is a power each of us possesses. Let me repeat that last line, for it represents the main theme of my talk. Humans own the unique power to select from a vast universe only those bits of information they find useful in making sense of the world in which they live.

I'm convinced our lives consist of a constant process of turning information into knowledge, but that each of us must determine for him or herself what constitutes that knowledge. Information without knowledge has no value. It is only when people select information units which are relevant to the knowledge they already possess or seek to develop that they attach a value to the information at all. Now if you find this hypothesis intellectually palatable, then you can understand why different people value different types of information. Machines are better at processing certain kinds of information units than others, but not all people attach equal value to those units, to that information. Not everyone finds the information relevant, not everyone considers it all useful in the process of making sense of his or her world. That's another point we need to keep in mind as we proceed into the future, fascinated by the potential that the technologies present us, and perhaps drawn by their promise for a better way of life.

What we perceive as knowledge--and we regard as knowledge that which helps us make sense of our world--will change over time as we progress from our first thoughts at birth, to our last thoughts at death. And it represents a life-long process. Sometimes a light bulb turns on in our minds as we resolve an anomaly or puzzle that has previously been perplexing us. We've all had those experiences, and often we consider them as watersheds in our lives. Thomas Kuhn has argued very persuasively that science does not show a nice smooth pattern of progress over time, but instead has moved by fits and starts, influenced in large part by the scientists's knowledge--the way he or she looks at the world, the way he or she makes sense of the data or information with which he or she is working. And that situation persists today. Current schools of thought concerning the unsolved puzzles in the sciences dictate in large part the directions which research will take, the agendas they will tend to follow, even though there is a great likelihood the direction being pursued will yield few results. All of the research now going on to cure AIDS seems to follow that pattern. No one *knows* a cure, and so the people working on the disease spend much time and energy--and money--trying to validate educated guesses. But despite failures we pursue anyway, until sometimes, in the near future we hope, someone will find the answer, someone will make sense of the problem.

Social scientists and humanists follow the same process, but so much of what they observe, so many of the questions they ask, come directly from the problems besetting the human condition as they perceive them in these last decades of the twentieth century. And constantly we must remind ourselves--the questions we are asking now will not be the questions future humanists and social scientists will ask a generation from now, just as they are not the same questions addressed by the generation preceding us.

All human beings process information, but they do so for the most part to reinforce existing knowledge. And each individual must make a determination for him or herself about the composition of that knowledge. Each of us in this room has a different perception of the world, each of us has a different perception of reality; here I hasten to remind you that Plato's observation--perception is reality--has the ring of truth.

Patrick Wilson has accurately observed, I think, that there are two kinds of knowledge. First-hand knowledge represents the learning that takes place as a direct result of what we experience. Most of us learned what "hot" means by this method. It certainly gave us an unforgettable lesson. But our first-hand experiences are not sufficient in number to allow us to cope in the modern world. They are certainly not numerous enough to allow us to make sense of all that is going on around us. Therefore, we have to rely very heavily upon second-hand knowledge, Wilson says, the kind we derive from the experiences of others. And this second-hand knowledge itself relies upon a body of information from which it has drawn its conclusions, and upon which it makes its claims to truth. Michel Foucault, a French moral philosopher, has argued persuasively, I think, that where the human condition is involved, truth is relative. There is no absolute truth, only truth-claims that vary in their ability to influence and persuade over time and place.

Scholars have discovered that the average human mind functions with seven to nine operating concepts. These concepts change over time, influenced in part by first-hand knowledge, but to a much larger extent by the persuasiveness of the second-hand knowledge with which we come in contact. The arguments we found persuasive at age six were different from those found persuasive at age 16, different from those we found persuasive at age 26, and certainly different from those we will find persuasive at age 66. Thus, we constantly shift those concepts over time in order to allow us to make sense of our world. And when we latch onto a set that taken together appears to solve the puzzles, taken together helps us make sense of our worlds, taken together seems to put our mind at ease and allows us to say to ourselves, "Hey, I finally figured it out," that's when we get much more comfortable. At this point in my own life, I find myself in one of those situations. In fact, the claim to truth about the library and information science profession currently swimming around in my head seems so convincing, makes so much sense to me, it probably gave me the courage to accept Al's invitation.

So, there are my ideas, and I throw them out to you at the end of this conference in the hope that it will remind us all, and certainly those in our profession, that there is indeed a delicate balance between people and information technology, and we ignore that balance only at our own professional peril. Constantly we need to remind ourselves that each individual will automatically turn information into knowledge in order to make sense of his or her own world. And the world is full of people who look upon reality in very different ways. We as information professionals have limited power to influence this process. Let me give you a few examples.

My grandfather died at the age of 102 believing that the world was square because the Bible very clearly said "four corners of the earth." No amount of arguments I made, no amount of scientific evidence I brought him fresh from my college classes, could convince him otherwise. His perception of Scripture, for most of the 102 years of his life, allowed him to make sense of his world, and for the most part dictated what data he drew from that vast world of information available to him. Certainly he was scientifically wrong, but the decisions he had to make in order to cope with life did not hinge on his accurate scientific perceptions. He was a member of a fundamentalist religious group of German peasants who had emigrated to Russia with Catherine the Great to raise her vegetables. The group seldom intermarried with the local Russian population. When the Revolution came in 1917, they were no longer welcome in Russia, and they could not return to Germany because of the war. One in ten made it through Ellis Island, ultimately settled in the Midwest, and regrouped their church. My grandfather's faith--however scientifically flawed--helped sustain him through those turbulent, dangerous times. It enabled him to cope with a set of circumstances which may have defeated someone whose perception of reality lacked a unified set of concepts enabling him or her to make sense of a very confusing world.

Or let's try another example perhaps more common to us all. I am sure there are a number of people in this room who are or have been parents of teenagers. I know everyone in this room was once a teenager him or herself. Have you ever tried to "reason" with a teenager? I am beginning to think that is an impossibility for an adult, in part because teenagers call upon different kinds of information when they begin to struggle with the need to make sense of their own worlds, however flawed we adults think their perceptions of reality are. I know I went through that stage, and a painful one it was for both my parents and me. And my wife and I watched each of our three children go through that same state; the youngest is now applying the finishing touches to that process.

Adults manifest a variety of ways of making sense of their worlds, and as a result they in large part predetermine the information units they select to reinforce or verify those seven to nine concepts which they have chosen or inherited by a social conditioning process, and by which they govern their lives. Again, Patrick Wilson is very helpful here. He points out that human beings gather unto themselves a group of "cognitive authorities" whose dictates they find very useful in making sense of their worlds. And recent scholarship bears him out, identifying a variety of operating concepts governing the average adult. Some social scientists have labelled these sets of concepts canons, others ideologies or paradigms, or, more recently, interpretive frames which tend to reproduce culture. And often applied to these clusters of concepts are the ideas of such powerful and persuasive cognitive authorities as Moses, Karl Marx, Jesus Christ, Sigmund Freud, Confucius, B. F. Skinner, Mohammed, or Antonio Gramsci, to name just a few--authorities whom million of people call upon as possessing the most plausible claim to truth, whose arguments have helped them make most sense of their worlds. And, of course, each group tends to select from that vast universe of information those units that tend to reinforce preconceived notions. If Kuhn found this to be the case for hard sciences, how much more is this true for students of the human condition?

And people get their information from all sorts of sources. Over the past several years I have developed an interest in the scholarship currently addressing popular culture, and especially the printed word in popular culture. This has taken me to reading the results of research on westerns, science fiction, and more recently, popular romances. A generation ago a very serious school of thought emerged in Germany which makes a convincing case that we need to address much more attention to the interaction taking place between the text and the reader, rather than trying to rediscover what the authors intended to say. Now if one concentrates attention on the interaction between text and reader, one senses echoes of that simple continuum which constitutes the central theme of my remarks. People *choose* the information they will turn into knowledge. And sure enough, the scholarship--many classify it as hermenutics scholarship--has discovered that people select from the text those elements they find most useful, most relevant to their own lives, and thus process the information in such a way to permit them to make sense of their worlds. And scholars of the popular arts who have built upon this truth claim the social sciences are finding the same things. I fully recommend to you a book by Janice Radway, entitled *Reading the Romance: Women, Patriarchy, and Popular Literature*, published by the University of North Carolina Press in 1984. Radway investigated the interaction taking place between readers of Harlequin romances and the texts of those romances in a Pennsylvania suburb. What she found out was fascinating; the criteria used by these avid readers to determine what was a good story and what was a bad story will seem very remote to a librarian who subscribes to collection development guidelines dictated by what others might call a high culture canon. But I hasten to remind you. Those readers are people who must make sense of their world just like you and me, just like my grandfather, just like my children. I know I have very little control over that process. I can certainly disagree with them all and argue that they are not drawing from the best information units upon which to base their day-to-day decisions, but I still can't force my point of view in this capitalist economy governed by a democratic form of government. And frankly, I wouldn't have it any other way. The women who are reading Harlequins in a Pennsylvania suburb are processing information from a body of data which helps them cope, which helps them make sense of their world. That is what Radway found out, and if you find those conclusions plausible, you will probably agree with me that her findings bear significant implications for us as a profession.

We also need to remember that our profession does represent at least one, but more likely several socioeconomic strata in contemporary society. As representatives of those strata, or that one stratum, we share similar ideas, parallel concepts by which we govern our lives. That's one of the things that draws us together. For example, we generally have found similar ways to turn information into knowledge. My guess is that everyone in this room has an undergraduate degree from an institution of higher education. That degree generally signals some acquaintance with and acceptance of certain cultural, literary, and intellectual canons, and reflects to some degree general consensus surrounding the process of making sense of our world. And we would probably also agree that literacy is essential, that books and libraries are necessary to a free world. But what about other issues? Not all of us agree that abortion is moral. But whatever side of each issue you may take, you *select* from the same universe of information as those taking opposing points of view.

Each human being must make sense of his or her own world, and in the process selects very carefully from that vast body of information available, and over which we claim concern and professional responsibility. But let us always remember, we do not own all the answers. We may not even own the best answers. Oh, we may own the best answers for ourselves, but we cannot claim to own the best answers for everyone. We can hope that the information we chose to acquire, store, and make available for retrieval will serve a lot of people, but I think we also have to be realistic enough to admit that the institutions we have set up to deal with information house only a fraction of the universe of information people use on a day-to-day basis. Statistics show that the vast majority have little or no direct need for these institutions we claim are essential. I think that represents evidence that most people draw from bodies of information outside our institutions in order to make sense of their worlds. Remember my grandfather. He never stepped foot in a library; he could easily have been lead by a librarian to a source of information which was scientifically accurate, but he wouldn't have believed it. And after all, what does it really matter? His perception of his world was determined by a set of concepts he had found very useful, a set which had allowed him to negotiate a tumultuous existent which drove him from Russia to this country at a time when no country wanted him. I could get very angry with him for acting upon what I considered misinformation, and yet he died a very happy human being, content that the set of concepts he had assembled over a century of life was right. And why should I bother to argue? His beliefs hurt no one, which perhaps is ultimately the only moral question I could apply to what I might consider flawed knowledge.

So now we come back to the task set up for me--"People and Technology: A Delicate Balance." I feel certain that we will create very sophisticated systems which will allow us to retrieve information rapidly and efficiently, and I applaud our profession's role in the cutting edge of this movement. But we constantly need to remind ourselves that each human being determines for him or herself what information will be turned into knowledge. Are we doing a good job of ensuring that a body of information to which we apply the developing technology is for the most part the information people want, or is it the information we believe, in perhaps a very prescriptive way, that people need? Let us not allow our fascination with the technology to dictate what information we decide to acquire, store, and make available for contemporary and future generations. Historians are just now developing the methodologies which are enabling us to discover and study whole subcultures previous generations have ignored, in part because the information specialists who were our professional forebears did not think the types of records these subcultures generated, the types of information sources from which they drew their knowledge, was worth preserving. Let's make sure that our fascination with the technology does not dictate what information we chose to collect, store, and retrieve, for fear we will be doing subsequent generations a disservice because of a set of professional blinders brought by the technology itself.